THE PASSION MANIFESTO

A PRACTICAL GUIDE TO ESCAPE THE RAT
RACE, UNCOVER YOUR PASSION AND DESIGN
A CAREER AND LIFE YOU LOVE

THIBAUT MEURISSE

CONTENTS

INTRODUCTION

Thank you for purchasing this book. I applaud your desire to make changes and design a life you don't want to escape from. As the saying goes, the journey of a thousand miles always starts with one single step. By reading this book, you have already taken this first step.

I will start by reminding you that you have the power to create your destiny and live the life you've designed, not the life someone else has designed for you. While a century ago there were only a few hundred jobs available, nowadays we can choose from thousands of different careers. In fact, according to Nicholas Lore, founder of the Rockport Institute, a center for career counseling, there are more than ten thousand careers available today which gives us ample scope to decide what we want to do for a living.

While many people despise their jobs, a significant number of people actually love what they do. The Rockport Institute's survey reveals that thirty percent either like or love their job. Among them, ten percent report they love their work. This means in the United States alone, millions of people love what they do to earn a living. So, if you have ever doubted your ability to design a career you love, remember these numbers. If millions of people have done it, you can do it as well.

The second step in your journey is simply to believe you can. Yes, you can attract the resources you need and develop the skills required to create your dream career. You can also overcome your self-defeating behaviors, and this book will help you do so.

I understand you may have to stay at a job you hate for a few years, but please don't be the person who stays at the same boring job for a working lifetime. Instead, realize that if you are in your mid-thirties and are still working at a dead-end job, it might be time to seriously question your career choices.

What if you decide today to take control of your life?

In this book, I invite you to redesign your career and align it with your aspirations, your unique strengths, and your personality. I encourage you to raise your standards and become the best you can be. Once you make the most of your strengths, talents, and personality, and overcome self-defeating behaviors, you will achieve more than you ever thought possible.

So, are you ready to find out what you love and make a living from it?

What you'll learn in this book

This book is a practical guide for dreamers. Its purpose is to help you discover what you love and actually earn a living from it. Life is too short to spend time doing things that don't inspire you.

More specifically, you will learn:

- How to find out who you really are and what you really love
- How to remove self-defeating behaviors and develop a winning mindset
- How to identify the very essence of your career goal and ensure you set the right goal for you
- How to create a detailed action plan to reach your goal
- How to find all the resources you need to make your goal a reality, and
- How to stay accountable and achieve your long-term goal.

Who this book is for

You will greatly benefit from this book if:

- You want to change jobs but are unsure what career to pursue
- You know what your ideal career is but don't know how to create it
- You have a vague dream and need help to gain clarity, and/or
- You have a dream and want to develop the mindset needed to make it a reality.

If you identify with any of the situations mentioned above, keep reading.

How to use this book

This book will help you identify your passion and create a specific long-term plan to design an exciting career around this passion. To extract the most value from this book, I encourage you to complete all the exercises in it. The more time and effort you to expend, the better your results will be.

I invite you to go through this book as many times as necessary until you absorb all the information you need to design your ideal career and life. Remember: repetition is the mother of mastery.

Make sure you download your Dream Career Action Guide. It includes all the exercises in the book and will guide you along your journey. For optimum results, I encourage you to print it out.

I also have other surprises waiting for you when you download the Guide so don't wait, download it now.

YOUR FREE DREAM CAREER ACTION GUIDE

Before we get started, make sure you download your free Dream Career Action Guide available at the following URL:

http://whatispersonaldevelopment.org/the-passion-manifesto

If you have any difficulties downloading the workbook contact me at:

thibaut.meurisse@gmail.com

and I will send it to you as soon as possible.

PART I
ADOPTING THE RIGHT MINDSET

1

WHY YOU SHOULD DO WHAT YOU LOVE

> *You've got to find what you love. And that is as true for your work as it is for your lovers. Your work is going to fill a large part of your life, and the only way to be truly satisfied is to do what you believe is great work. And the only way to do great work is to love what you do. If you haven't found it yet, keep looking. Don't settle. As with all matters of the heart, you'll know when you find it. And, like any great relationship, it just gets better and better as the years roll on. So, keep looking until you find it. Don't settle.*
>
> — STEVE JOBS.

Why should you do what you love? Let me ask it another way: Why *shouldn't* you do what you love?

Do you intend to spend your entire life at a job that doesn't fulfill you? Does waking up depressed every Monday morning sound like a good life plan to you?

If so, I invite you to think differently.

Most people buy into the myth that after decades of hard work, they'll be able to retire and finally enjoy their lives. This is a terrible idea. Retirement is a trap. By believing retirement is paradise on earth, you tacitly accept your present condition. You suffer now, hoping to reap the rewards later. This may be a great idea if you're a passionate entrepreneur and later means five years from now, but not so much if you're an employee and later means thirty-five years from now! This thinking can lead you to sacrifice a large part of your life, and there is no guarantee you will retire as a healthy person, anyway. You may not even live long enough to retire. Who knows! It may be likely, but it is definitely *not* guaranteed.

Forget about retirement for now. Instead, ask yourself the following question, "If, for any reason, I could never retire and had to work until the day I die, would I still be doing what I'm doing right now?"

If you answered "no," I'm afraid you may have to change something. Don't worry, that's what we'll work on in this book.

What about financial freedom? It's a wonderful idea, isn't it?

Well, even this idea needs to be challenged.

Internet entrepreneur, Dan Lok, believes financial freedom is an illusion. Instead, he prefers to use the term financial confidence. Without doubt, technologies evolve, financial crashes occur, and new competitors arise all the time. Thus, the most important thing is not to have enough money to stop working, but to have enough skills to never have to worry about making money again. Have you noticed rich people often make their money back quickly after a bankruptcy? Why do you think this is the case? I would argue it's largely because they have both the skills and the mindset to create wealth.

Who cares whether financial freedom is an illusion? What you want is to make enough money and retire, right?

This is yet another myth to bust: the idea that once you've made enough money, you'll retire on the beach drinking Piña Colada and live happily ever after. Have you ever seen billionaires quitting their jobs to relax on the beach and 'finally' enjoy life? No. In fact, often billionaires don't ever retire. What does that tell you?

The internet entrepreneur Dan Lok was so excited when, at the tender age of twenty-seven, he finally 'made it.' He'd become a millionaire and didn't have to work a day for the rest of his life. What more could he have hoped for? After all, he had achieved the dreams of millions of people around the world. Isn't this why people keep playing the lottery?

The first day after he retired, Mr. Lok travelled to English Bay in Vancouver where he lay on the beach while drinking a tasty fruit punch. He thought, "This is cool. This is really nice!" He enjoyed the beach for a few more weeks but the excitement progressively wore off and after thirty days, he was bored out of his mind.

"This is nuts. I can't do this. I worked so hard to get to this point where I got here. I was looking at the beach, I'm like, this is not what I signed up for. This is not what I wanted. This is not how life is supposed to be," —Dan Lok.

What did he do next?

Well, he happened to be a big movie fan. He decided to stay at home and watch movies all day long. Who doesn't like to watch movies while eating their favorite snacks? Thirty days later, he was bored and unhappy again. He couldn't understand what was wrong with him. In despair, he called his mentor, who had been in the same position. I'm sure you can guess what his mentor advised?

To go back to work, which Mr. Lok did.

So, why am I talking about retirement and financial freedom as being a trap? Why does it even matter?

The concept is important for two main reasons. First, people who buy into the myth of financial freedom tend to believe they have to make more money to retire early—and finally enjoy their lives. As a result, they may choose the wrong careers spending years at jobs they absolutely hate. Second, they may lack the patience required to create a meaningful career they genuinely love. Because they believe in the myths of (early) retirement and financial freedom, they may focus most of their efforts on saving or making more money, instead of taking time to design their ideal career.

Now, wouldn't it be easier if you commit to doing something you love so much you'll probably never even *want* to retire? You wouldn't need to make that much money. You would likely dedicate more time to designing your ideal career and life. Rather than rushing to change your career, you could spend years meticulously gathering pieces together until you craft you ideal career. You would be more likely to learn new skills and set clear conditions both pre and post-retirement. For instance, you might decide to work forty to fifty hours per week until age sixty and only fifteen or twenty hours per week after that. Or you might come up with ways to plan long breaks during your career.

All these things are possible if you give yourself enough time to plan your life properly. I truly believe you should spend the right amount of time thinking about the life you want to create for yourself and then, spend as much time as you can putting the pieces of the puzzle together. With a clear vision and a total commitment to creating your ideal career and life, you can make drastic changes in a very short time.

However, in reality, most people actually spend more time writing their grocery list than setting goals and designing their life plan. They fail to realize life is a long-term strategy game. To 'win' the game and live life on your own terms, you must set your priorities straight. These priorities are:

1) Knowing yourself: your personality, core values, strengths, and talent

2) Deciding exactly what you want, and

3) Spending the rest of your life doing what it takes to create your ideal life.

This is the objective I had in mind when writing this book. Once you understand yourself, decide what you want and take action towards your goal every day, you can transform your life in ways you can't even begin to imagine. So why do most people ignore this three-step-process and wander aimlessly through life instead?

It's a mystery to me.

Remember, you have everything you need within you to create the life of your dreams. In today's world, you are virtually one click away from countless people who can help you change your life. Importantly, you also have access to most of the world's knowledge and, best of all, much of this knowledge is free or available at a very low cost.

So, are you committed to finding out what you love and to making it happen?

2

UNCOVERING YOUR ASSUMPTIONS ABOUT LIFE

We all hold beliefs that limit us in some way or another—often unconsciously. Sometimes, just one or two false beliefs can affect our entire life, preventing us from living the life we want. I call these beliefs "life assumptions."

A common assumption is "life is hard," and without doubt, millions of people are struggling right now. But is life really hard? Is it the truth or merely a belief? If it is true, how come so many people enjoy life for the most part?

Now, if you believe life is hard, how does this belief affect your emotions and the actions you take? What are the consequences of adopting this negative belief?

To a large extent, your beliefs create your reality. When you assume life is hard, you constantly look for evidence to prove it and, sure enough, you'll find plenty. But is this the most effective way to live your life?

I prefer to make the assumption that "life is easy." Then, whenever I'm struggling, I'll ask myself how I may be making my life harder than it actually is. I must have decided to hold onto beliefs or behaviors that contribute to making it that way.

Do you understand how changing just one of your assumptions can drastically affect your life?

Let me give you one more example.

In 2009, I came to Japan to work at a prefectural office as part of the 'JET program.' My job entailed translating official documents and pamphlets, visiting schools to introduce French culture, and organizing events. Many of my friends in the program enjoyed their work and I tried to convince myself that I did too. Yet, deep down, I wasn't really passionate about the work.

One day, as I was chatting to one of my supervisors, he said he perceived work as a way to make a living, nothing more. He believed there wasn't any need to enjoy our job and that we should just enjoy our lives outside of work. At the time, I thought he might be right. After all, he was much older than I was. I had been working for less than a year while he had thirty years of work experience. Perhaps, it wasn't possible for me to find a job I loved. If so, maybe I should just show up to work, do what I was told, and go home to enjoy my life. But something didn't seem quite right to me. I couldn't accept that 'fact.' And I didn't.

Now, imagine what would have happened if I had bought into the assumption that we can't—and aren't supposed to—enjoy our work. This assumption alone would have prevented me from chasing my dreams and creating a career I love. Unfortunately, I suspect many people live their lives with this same, erroneous assumption—and many others—running through the back of their mind. What about you? What are your assumptions about work? And what could be the consequences?

Another major assumption we have is in regard to our potential.

Most of us massively underestimate what we can accomplish. As a result, we doubt ourselves and settle for far less than we're capable of achieving. To create our ideal life, it is necessary we remove this erroneous assumption and believe we can achieve our goals.

* * *

Action step

Write down some of your assumptions using the free Dream Career Action Guide. (*Part 1. Uncovering your assumptions*) To give you a start, some common examples are:

- I can't make a living doing what I love.
- I can't make as much money as with my current job.
- Work isn't supposed to be fun.

Now, what if the opposite were true?

Create a turnaround statement to start loosening your beliefs. How does that make you feel? Do you feel some inner resistance?

- Work isn't supposed to be fun —> Work *is* supposed to be fun
- I can't make a living doing what I love —> I *can* make a living doing what I love
- I can't make as much money as with my current job —> I *can* make more money doing what I love than doing what I'm currently doing

3

BELIEVING YOU CAN

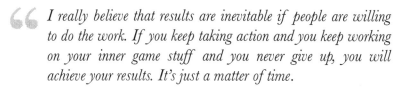 *I really believe that results are inevitable if people are willing to do the work. If you keep taking action and you keep working on your inner game stuff and you never give up, you will achieve your results. It's just a matter of time.*

— CHRISTIAN MICKELSEN, AUTHOR AND COACH.

Most of what you accomplish in life results from your level of belief in yourself and in your vision. Belief is the invisible force that changes the visible world.

Now, let me ask you a simple question. Do you believe you can change your career? Do you truly believe you can find a job you love and make a living from your passion?

I believe you can. I also believe you already know the answer at an intuitive level. Now, my goal throughout this book is to turn your answer into a big, "Of course, I can. And I will."

What does it really take to find what you love and make a living from it?

Have you ever wondered why some people achieve their goals while others fail? Here is the secret: the successful ones made it a *must*. They are committed to making it happen. They didn't 'hope' it would happen; they didn't wish for it to happen; they didn't think, "it would be nice if it happened." No, they decided it *will* happen.

What about you? Are you committed to creating your ideal career or are you merely interested?

If you're merely "interested," you'll try making changes in your life for a few months, and when things don't work out as planned you'll give up. But when you're totally committed, you'll do whatever it takes to make it happen. You won't give up until you achieve the results you really want. It might take more time than you thought—it usually does—but you will eventually generate the results you want.

In short, if you're *interested*, you'll probably fail, but if you're *committed*, you'll likely succeed.

Do you want to quit your boring job and create your own business? Commit to it.

Do you want to work from home so that you can spend more time with your kids? Resolve to make it happen.

Do you want to change your career and find a more exciting job? Decide to do it.

The act of committing may not sound very practical to you, but it is one of the most practical things you can do. Committing—like believing—is using the invisible (your mind) to create the visible (an exciting career). Unless you commit, none of the content in this book or in any other books of its type will help you create the exciting career you seek.

* * *

Action step

Rate your level of commitment using your Dream Career Action
Guide. (*Part 1. - Believing you can*)

4

TAKING ONE HUNDRED PERCENT RESPONSIBILITY

W. Clement Stone, the mentor of the motivational speaker Jack Canfield, once asked him whether he was taking one hundred percent responsibility for his life? When Jack Canfield replied, "I think so", Mr. Stone went on saying, "This is a yes or no question, young man. You either do or you don't."

What about you? Are you taking one hundred percent responsibility for your life? Have you ever blamed someone else for any given circumstance in your life? Have you ever complained about anything? If so, I'm afraid you aren't taking full responsibility.

Taking full responsibility for your life means you refuse to blame other people or circumstances for your lack of results. You accept you're entirely responsible for both your success *and* your failure in any area of your life including your career. After all, you are at your current job because you chose to, whether by personal choice or by default, (by failing to decide otherwise). Did your parents, your friends or society "force" you to become a doctor, a lawyer or an engineer? No. You choose to let people dictate your life. You choose to meet other people's needs and not yours.

One of my father's friends became a dentist to please his father who was a doctor. He didn't want to be a dentist. To make things worse, he was a southpaw and had to learn to use his right hand instead. Can you imagine excavating a cavity using your 'wrong' hand? Instead, he would have loved to be a bartender. Now, what prevents him from doing that? Nothing. Or should I say, his father does. Or rather, he allows his father to make the decision for him.

What about you? Are you doing what you want to do or what someone else expects of you?

To take full responsibility you must eliminate all excuses. Some common excuses are:

- I'm too old.
- I'm too young.
- I'm not smart enough.
- I don't know the right people.
- I don't have the right education.
- I don't have enough experience.
- I don't know how to do it.
- I don't have enough time.
- My father/mother won't approve of it, and
- There is too much competition.

Do you know why you love your excuses so much? It's because you can use them to bury the truth and avoid making changes in your life. Doing nothing but complaining is much easier than solving your issues.

However, blaming circumstances and people has severe consequences: it prevents you from living the life you desire. By not taking responsibility, you give your power away to people and circumstances and say goodbye to your dreams. Remember that you can *either* make excuses *or* make your dreams a reality.

So, would you rather keep your excuses or design a career you love?

A final note: Taking responsibility doesn't mean blaming yourself. That would be playing the victim to avoid making changes, which is the opposite of taking responsibility. No, it means acknowledging you have your part of the responsibility and accept that, for things to change, *you* have to change.

Being the creator of your life

"If you don't design your own life plan, chances are that you'll fall into someone else's plan. And guess what they have planned for you? Not much," —Jim Rohn, entrepreneur and motivational speaker.

You have much more control over your destiny than you imagine. You're not a powerless creature as politicians or the media would like you to believe. You're the creator of your own destiny. At any moment, you can decide to change your life.

Every new day presents opportunities for you to make choices that will shape your destiny. Did you know that, on average, people make over 35,000 decision each day? For instance, it is you who decides to:

- Wake early or hit the snooze button
- Watch TV or work on your side business
- Read business/self-help books or read comics
- Get drunk all weekend or work toward your goals
- Eat healthily or choose junk food
- Focus on the positive or dwell on the negative
- Set specific goals or wander through life aimlessly, and/or
- Fritter away all your money or invest it wisely.

Now, what would happen if you were to make just a few different choices each day? What if you spent thirty minutes working on your side business or reading educational books? What difference would that make over six months, one year or one decade?

If you feel stuck, it is likely because you're caught up into the same old story that has been holding you back for years. Perhaps, you don't believe you deserve success and even doubt you can ever change. Or maybe you believe you don't know the right people? But is that really true?

Remember that you're not a robot. You don't have to keep reading the same story. You don't have to repeat this year the same as last year. You can revise your plan, take different actions and achieve different results. The key is to be proactive and to stop waiting for people to come to you or for things to happen. Instead, you must act as the creator of your life which means:

1. Don't expect to be given a job. It is your responsibility to go after what you want and make it happen. Refuse to believe society owes you a job because you went to university, because your friends have a job or for any other reason. Instead, take full responsibility. Nobody but you can design your ideal career. Don't be the person who says, "nobody will give me a job."

2. Learn about yourself. Knowing your personality, strengths, talents and passions is essential. Take time to learn about yourself. Ask people around you to help you identify your strengths. Work with a career coach or take personality tests. Learn to trust yourself and move towards your dream. If you're in the wrong job or don't know what to do, start by acknowledging you're not where you want to be. Then, commit to learning more about yourself and finding what you want to do.

3. Always think of ways to add value. Put yourself in the shoes of potential employers and answer the following question with brutal honesty: "If I were this employer would I hire a person like me?" If you answered no, think of ways you could turn the "No" into a "Yes." Then ask yourself, "What kind of person would I need to become to be hired for my dream job? What would I need to bring to the table?"

4. Constantly learn. Never stop growing and continuously strive to develop skills that will allow you to land your dream job. Never stop learning, and make sure you read every day. If you're unemployed, avoid wasting time watching TV. Instead, use your precious time to learn valuable new skills. All successful people are life-long learners. You should be, too.

5. Ask yourself the right questions. Most people ask themselves the wrong questions and, as a result, come up with the wrong answers. As the famous life coach, Tony Robbins said, the quality of your questions determines the quality of your life. Instead of asking yourself questions such as "Why can't I find a job?" or "Why is this so hard?" ask yourself empowering questions such as:

- Why is it so important to me?
- What kind of person do I need to become in order to spend the rest of my life doing what I love?
- How can I make money doing what I love?
- What could I do today that would move me closer to my dream?
- What one skill if I were to develop would help me achieve my goal?
- Who can I learn from?
- Who could help me achieve my goal?
- Who has achieved what I want and how did they do it?

6. Focus on what you want. Think about what you want repeatedly throughout the day. Visualize what it would look like to live your passion and resolve to do what it takes to make it happen.

7. Don't give up. Once you decide to spend the rest of your life doing what you love, you refuse to give up prematurely. You don't abandon your goals after sending 100, 500 or even 1,000 resumes. You do not throw the towel after a few months or even a few years. Instead, you're ready to work at it until you end up exactly where you want to be.

8. Don't rely on luck. Instead, do everything in your power to achieve your goal. If you're taking job interviews, thoroughly research the companies you're applying for. Accept the fact it is your responsibility to learn how to nail job interviews. Read as many books, watch as many videos, and practice as many times as needed until you become great at it. Seek advice offline on online from the best teachers in the field. Ask your network of friends for help, cold call companies and even ask to work for free if needed. Do what it takes to get a foot in the door and eventually you will succeed.

* * *

Action step

Assess how much responsibility you're taking using your action (Part 1. - *Taking one hundred percent responsibility for your life/You're the creator of your life*).

5

FACING THE TRUTH

The importance of absolute honesty

> *The key that unlocks the prison of external expectations is the willingness to tell the truth to yourself, to your family and friends, and to the whole word. Your gut feeling should be what is in the driver's seat, not other people's expectations.*
>
> — CHERIE CARTER-SCOTT, IF SUCCESS IS A GAME, THESE ARE THE RULES.

The first step to finding out what you love is to acknowledge your current situation with complete honesty. Unless you're absolutely honest with yourself, you cannot change. You often have a vested interest in lying to yourself as it can be hard to admit that the job you've been doing for years is miles away from what you really want to do. Let me ask you a straightforward question:

Do you love your job?

What did you answer? Did you immediately answer with a big

"Yes?" or did you hesitate even just a fraction of a second? Perhaps, you answered one of the following:

- It's fine.
- I'm not complaining.
- Things could be worse.
- It's not perfect but …

Be honest with yourself. If you'd rather do something else, admit it. For now, don't worry about the practicality of your dreams, just look at your current situation and ask yourself whether it is what you want.

Knowing why you do what you do

Why are you working at your current job? Who sold you on the plan, and is it working?

Did you choose your current career to make your parents proud of you or to make money? Or was it because you didn't believe you could land your ideal job? Or perhaps you just didn't know what to do?

It is essential for you to know why you are where you are now and to take responsibility for being there. While your parents or society may have influenced you, you still had free will. You could have chosen a different path, but you didn't.

Trusting yourself

Sadly, nowadays most people rely solely on their intellect, hoping their mind will give them the solution they need. Then, they wonder why they aren't happy once they achieved everything society told them they should want. While your intellect is a powerful tool that can allow you to achieve extraordinary things, it cannot really help you find out what you want. Nor can your family, your friends or society.

To find out what you're supposed to do with your life, you need to learn how to trust your intuition. At an intuitive level, you understand your strengths, personality, talents, and preferences and know what you should be doing. It might not be crystal clear yet, but if you're honest enough with yourself, I suspect you'll at least have some ideas.

What does your intuition tell you?

* * *

Action step

Answer the questions in your Dream Career Action Guide (*Part 1. - Facing the truth*)

PART II

FINDING OUT WHO YOU ARE

6

KNOWING YOUR PERSONALITY

How well do you know yourself? Are you an extrovert or an introvert? Do you belong to a tribe or are you a maestro? What are your biggest strengths and natural talents?

The truth is, while we can use the extraordinary power of our mind to learn whatever skills we need, we all have different personalities, and these need to be taken into account when designing both our careers, and our lives in general.

Have you ever found yourself struggling at work, feeling you aren't doing what you're supposed to? This is probably due to you being in the wrong environment. Perhaps, the job in itself is okay, but you need more privacy or, on the contrary, more opportunities to interact with people. Or maybe you value autonomy and hate being micro-managed by your boss. It could also be your job is out of sync with your deepest values or interests. That's what happens when your job isn't aligned with your personality.

Learning more about your personality will help you make better choices and design a career that works for you.

The major components of your personality

In this section, we'll talk about the major components of your personality. For simplicity purpose, I've divided your personality into the following categories:

- Your innate talent, (what you're naturally good at)
- Your energy type, (how you spend your energy)
- Your core values, (what matters the most to you), and
- Your relationships with others, (how you relate to others).

Now, let's dive into each of them.

Note that all the exercises in this section are included in your action guide. If you haven't yet, make sure you download it here (*add link)

1. Your innate talent

Do you know what your talents are and what makes you unique? We all have specific talents and things that we are naturally good at.

Highly successful people are good at identifying their core strengths and innate talents and are able to use this knowledge to design their careers. Instead of focusing solely on their weaknesses, they spend a considerable amount of time and effort improving their strengths and polishing their talent to become world-class at what they do.

If you're struggling at your current job, feeling you're not making a difference or not being good enough, you're probably not utilizing your natural talents well enough. I know from personal experience that spending time doing something you're bad at and don't enjoy can be extremely exhausting and extraordinarily depressing.

Your innate talent is also known as your 'zone of genius.' You want to operate from this place as much as possible. Your zones of genius are those areas in life that come to you so easily they don't feel like work. These activities are so effortless you can't even understand how others may have such a hard time doing the same things. Another good indicator you're operating from your zone of genius is when you dismiss compliments as it being no big deal. It might not be a big deal for you, but for many people, it is.

So, what are your zones of genius? What are you naturally good at and enjoy doing? The exercises below will help you identify your innate talent(s). Take the time to work this through. Without knowing what you're great at, you'll struggle to design your perfect career.

Exercise 1 - Write down your talents

Create a list of all your talents. Try to come up with at least ten. Don't worry if you're unsure. Write whatever comes to mind and don't dismiss anything you consider not worth mentioning. Maybe you're good at reading people, talking to people, building things with your hands, coming up with great ideas, learning, painting or making people laugh. Whatever they may be, write them down. To guide you consider asking yourself the following questions:

- What come so easily to me that I can't understand why other people struggle to do the same thing?
- What doesn't seem like work to me, although it is for other people?
- What is my unique talent? What is it only I can do?
- What activities can I lose myself in for hours?
- What am I often complimented for?

- What am I doing/talking about when I feel the most energized?

Look at your list and try to identify activities you both love doing *and* at which you excel.

Exercise 2 - Ask people around you

Often, your innate talents seem so natural, you are blind to the obvious. Asking people who know you what your talents are can be a real eye-opener. Make a list of people who know you well. Include your family, friends and colleagues. Send them an email and ask them some of the following questions:

- What is my unique gift?
- What are the three qualities you admire the most about me?
- What am I doing or talking about when I seem the most energized, happy and confident?
- What would you miss most about my presence if I passed away?

2. Your energy type

This is how you expend your energy. That is, whether you're an extrovert or an introvert. Extroverts feel energized when in presence of other people or in a stimulating environment. They usually enjoy parties and other social gatherings. Conversely, introverts are most energized from having meaningful conversations with a limited number of people or by spending time alone. Many introverts are also turned on by ideas. They tend to prefer quieter environments and, when interacting with people, feel more at ease in small groups.

Knowing whether you're an extrovert or an introvert will help you design a better work environment and choose a career that best suits your personality. Even if you don't change jobs, redesigning your environment to make it match your personality can boost your performance and enhance your well-being.

Bear in mind, extroversion and introversion exist on the same spectrum. This means there are various degrees of extroversion and introversion. People who falls in the middle of the spectrum are called ambiverts.

Below are some characteristics of extroverts and introverts.

Introverts:

- Spend time alone to replenish themselves
- Dislike small talk but enjoy deep conversation
- Prefer small groups
- Think before they speak
- Require an invitation before they speak
- Avoid speaking until they feel they have something important to say
- Listen more than they talk
- Talk a lot when the topic is something they're passionate about
- Choose depth over breadth, (they would rather know a few people very well than know several people casually)
- Keep their enthusiasm and excitement to themselves and share only with people they know very well
- Prefer to know a lot about a small cluster of topics than know a little bit about a wide range of topics
- Need alone time to think, (rather than having to endure brainstorming sessions)
- Dislike interruptions
- Be uncomfortable with conflict, and
- Need a lot of preparation before addressing an audience and have difficulties speaking for long periods of time.

Extroverts:

- Talk first and refine their thinking, (talking allows them to organize their ideas)
- Love talking with people
- Usually talk more than they listen
- Like teamwork
- Like to solve problems by discussing them
- Feel energized when they mingle with other people
- Enjoy being the center of attention
- Feel isolated by too much time spent alone, and
- Enjoy talking about a variety of different topics.

Whether you're an extrovert or an introvert will impact some of your decision, such as:

- Whether you want to work alone or with other people
- Whether you prefer an open space or want your own office, (or would prefer to work from home)
- Whether you want to interact with a lot of customers or be in the back office
- Whether you want to work in a loud or in a quiet environment
- Whether you prefer written or oral communication as your main means of communication, and
- Whether you prefer to brainstorm in team or by yourself.

Note that being an extrovert or an introvert doesn't exclude you from certain jobs. It just means you may have to take a different approach to your career. You can be an introvert and a great salesman, politician or actor. Similarly, you can be an extrovert and an excellent writer, artist or software programmer. The key here is whether or not you like your job.

If you're an introvert or want to learn more about introversion, I highly encourage you to refer to my book, *The Thriving Introvert: Embrace The Gift of Introversion and Live the Life You Were Meant to Live.*

3. Your core values

Do you know what matters the most to you? Could you give me your top five values right now? Knowing your core values and what you stand for is essential as it will help ensure you live a life aligned with who you really are.

Characteristics of values

We all use the word "values," but what does it really mean? Before you start identifying your core values it is important we take the time to understand, in detail, what values are and why they matter.

What values are

Put it simply, your values are ideals that matter most to you. These are non-negotiable things you can't do without. You live by them every day, or at least strive to live by them as much as possible. Living out of sync with your core values will erode your self-esteem, reduce your joy and negatively impact your level of motivation. Thus, a career that doesn't allow you to live by your most important values will most likely create stress, frustration and lead to unhappiness. When defining your values, it is important you remember the following:

Your values should be specific. Perhaps, you stated that freedom matters most to you. Or maybe you value safety over anything else. If so, what you do mean exactly when you say "freedom" or "safety"? Your definition of freedom is likely to differ from mine.

For example, freedom could be:

- Being self-employed and not having a boss telling you what to do
- Having the ability to take a vacation whenever you want, or
- Having a lot of autonomy at work.
- Safety could mean:
- Working for the government with little or no risk of being sacked
- Living in a neighborhood where you can go out at any time of the day or the night without fearing for your safety, or
- Having the confidence in your ability to switch jobs or easily find a new job because of the experience and the skills you have developed over the years.

As you can see, the same words can mean different things to different people.

Your values should be non-negotiable. Because your core values are what matter the most to you, they naturally act as guiding principles for your life. This means, when you face situations that challenge your values, you stand firm by those values. For instance, if honesty is your most important value, you'll go the extra mile to ensure your behaviors and decisions are congruent with that value.

If freedom—manifesting as being self-employed—is your most important value, you'll fight hard to maintain or create that situation. You'll work for someone else only if you have no choice or if it is part of your long-term goal to become self-employed, (the desire to learn a new skill or gain experience for instance).

The bottom line is that values are something you naturally strive to live by. Your values aren't:

- Things you believe you *should* do, (which implies external pressure to conform to something you aren't naturally drawn towards).

- Dreams and desires, (which implies things you aren't living by right now).

Three reasons why knowing your core values is key to your long-term success

Now, let's look in more depth at some reasons why knowing your core values is essential. Knowing your core values allows you to:

1. Focus on what you want most of the time: Once you know exactly what you stand for, you can design your life around it and spend most of your time making sure you live up to these values. You'll find it easier to say no to anything that doesn't match your values and you won't become distracted by projects out of sync with those values.

2. Make better decisions more quickly: This ties in to the first point. Once you have a clear vision and specific values to guide you, making decisions becomes easier. Whenever you need to make a major decision, you can simply check whether it matches your values. Should you take that job? Well, let's look at your values. For instance, if your number one value is freedom, taking a 9-5 job that offers no flexibility might not be the best option for you.

3. Experience more fulfillment and meaning in your life: When you live your life according to your core values, you experience a deeper sense of integrity. You know you're doing what you're supposed to do. As a result, you feel more at peace and you find life more meaningful.

In short, your core values are your guiding principles. They are what you stand for and they help you determine what actions to take at any given moment.

Exercise - identify your top ten values

In this exercise we will work on identifying your core values. I could give you a list of possible values to choose from, but I would like you to come up with your own list of values first. I don't want my list to influence your answers.

Avoid choosing values merely because they are noble or make you look or feel good. This exercise is for *you* only. Nobody needs to see or know your values. Do your best to be as honest as possible. Now, take a pen and piece of paper—or use the Dream Career Action Guide—and come up with at least ten values. Once you have your list, prioritize your values by giving them a number from 1 to 10—1 being the most important.

Once you have your list, you can refine it by looking at the following list of values available here, (add list of values).

Note that, while core values tend to be stable over time, they may change as you grow and evolve. Your priorities may change as well. It is possible for instance that, while your family is important to you, it is not your number 1 priority right now. It could very well be in a few years though.

Now, for each value, describe how you want to live by it in one sentence. As an example, below are my top ten values:

1. **Truth**: I'm constantly seeking the truth because progress is impossible without it. Awareness is a prerequisite to change.
2. **Integrity**: I don't do things I believe to be wrong, even if everyone else is doing them or refusing to do them will have negative consequences.
3. **Passion**: I'm passionate about what I do. I follow the passion in my everyday life, regardless of the challenges I face.
4. **Health**: I look after my health, as I want to feel good, be energized, live longer, and accomplish many things.
5. **Freedom**: I do what I like and am free to change my

job, travel, have the career I desire, and live without someone else calling the shots.

6. **Selflessness**: I help those around me, regardless of whether we're friends or how much they do or don't like me.
7. **Courage**: I face my fears to improve myself, unleash my true potential, and become the real me.
8. **Fairness**: I always try to be fair with people and avoid giving inequitable advantages to friends or family.
9. **Progress**: I feel joy in improving myself and learning new skills. I also encourage others to do the same.
10. **Uniqueness**: I'm unique and shouldn't be afraid to stand out or do things that truly matter to me.

4. Interpersonal relationship

How do you relate to others? Are you more competitive or more cooperative than most? Understanding your personality traits may help you answer these questions and further clarify what your ideal career could be.

Tribal vs. Maestro

Do you prefer working with others or would you rather work on your own? Nicholas Lore in his excellent book, *The Pathfinder,* suggests there are two types of people: Tribals or Maestros. Tribal people like to work for an organization and thrive when working with others towards a common goal.

Maestros, on the other hand, are the specialists. As Nicholas put it, *"a Maestro without a specialty is like a cat without claws, a bird without wings."* Maestros like to be experts in a specific area and they derive a large part of their identity from what they do as opposed to the organization they belong to. Thus, it is essential they choose something they are passionate about.

Please note, this doesn't mean Tribals are extroverts and Maestros introverts.

Tribals don't necessarily enjoy interacting with people all day long or working in a team. However, they are comfortable being part of a group of people who strive to achieve a common goal. Rather than focusing on mastering a specific skill, they enjoy doing a variety of activities and don't mind moving from job to job within an organization.

What about you? Do you see yourself as a Tribal or a Maestro? And do you fully express that aspect of your personality at your current job? If not, what could you start doing to behave more like one or the other?

Make sure you choose a career that allows you embrace your Tribal/Maestro personality. Otherwise, you may end up at an unfulfilling job that doesn't suit your personality.

Cooperation vs. Competition

The Big Five Personality Traits is a personality test that categorize people according to the following personality traits:

1. **Openness**: intellectually curious, creative, prefer novelty and variety, (opposite: consistent/cautious)
2. **Consciousness**: motivated, persistent, self-disciplined, reliable, (opposite: easy-going)
3. **Extroversion**: outgoing, talkative, assertive, sociable, (opposite: solitary/reserved)
4. **Agreeableness**: friendly, compassionate, cooperative, (opposite: competitive, challenging)
5. **Neuroticism**: sensitive, susceptible to negative emotions, insecure, easily stressed, (opposite: secure, confident)

People who score on the high end of agreeableness are more

prone to cooperate with other people and are more social. On the other hand, people who score low tend to be more competitive, callous or ill-tempered. Whether you score high or low on agreeableness affects your career choice, at least to some extent.

What do you enjoy the most? Cooperation or competition? How do you want that to be reflected in your career?

Action step:

Complete the exercises in your action guide (Part 2. Finding out who you are using your action guide).

To go further:

I encourage you to spend time learning about yourself. You can find popular personality tests online. If you want to delve deeper, you can also take more comprehensive tests, (usually paid tests). Below are some tests you might want to take:

- Big 5 Personality Test
- HEXACO
- Introversion/Extroversion
- Myer Briggs Test

In addition, I recommend the following book: *StrengthsFinder 2.0* by Tom Rath.

PART III

DISCOVERING WHAT YOU WANT

7

WHAT DO YOU REALLY WANT?

One of the main reasons people don't get what they want is because they have yet to identify their goals! If vague goals promote vague results, extreme clarity creates great results.

While your mind tends to think abstractly, your subconscious mind unleashes its full power only when it receives clear instructions. This is why the most important thing you can do to change your life is to decide exactly what you want.

So, what *do* you want?

What do you want to do for a living? How much money do you want to make? Where do you want to live? How many days to you want to work per week? How many hours? Do you want long vacations? If so, how long? What does your ideal day look like? At what time do you want to wake up? What skills do you want to develop? What emotions do you want to experience more of? What does your 'best self' look like? What's the deadline by which you must achieve this vision? When will you start?

All the exercises in this section are included in your action guide.

Exercise - What you really want

- Spend up to ten minutes to write down everything you want—whether or not it is related to your professional life.

- Select ten things you *really, really* want

- Write down the emotional value behind each thing you want. To do so you can use Tony Robbins' six human needs as a baseline. The six needs are:

1. **Certainty**: The need for security
2. **Uncertainty**: The need for variety in your life
3. **Significance**: The need to feel like you matter
4. **Connection/love**: The need to connect with people and feel loved
5. **Growth**: The need for personal growth
6. **Contribution**: The need to make a difference in the world

Alternatively, you can write down whatever values seem relevant to these things you want, (freedom, family, integrity, uniqueness etc.)

Exercise - Your dream career

Write down what your ideal career would look like using the questions below to help you:

- How many hours/days per week would I work?
- What would my ideal day look like and how would that make me feel?
- How much money would I make?
- How much vacation would I take and how often?
- Where would I be living?

Action step

Refer to the exercises in your action guide (*Part 3. - What do you really want?*)

8

FINDING OUT WHAT YOU LOVE

> *Tiger Woods loves to play golf. Ellen DeGeneres loves to make people laugh. My sister, Kimberly Kirberger, loves to design and make jewelry. Donald Trump loves to make deals and build buildings. I love to read and share what I have learned with others in books, speeches, and workshops. It is possible to make a living doing what you love.*
>
> — JACK CANFIELD, AUTHOR AND MOTIVATIONAL SPEAKER.

What if you love watching TV while eating potato chips? Does doing what you love mean you should look for ways to make money from doing that? While nowadays you can make money in surprising ways—from blogging about basketball to selling pasta online—you must be smart in your choice of career and differentiate mere hobbies from solid career ideas.

Doing what you love means knowing your strengths, talents, personality, and preferences, and combining

them in such a way that you spend most of your day doing something you're passionate about. Love means feeling deep inside what you're doing, what you're supposed to do and being positive about it, rather than struggling every day and wondering whether you will stay at a job you hate for the next forty years.

What do you love?

Do you know what you love? Can you clearly articulate your passions? If not, the exercises in this section will help. To uncover your true passions, let's start by gathering some valuable clues. More specifically, we will look at the following:

1. Twenty things you love the most
2. What you focus on and think about most often
3. What you prefer to do in your spare time
4. What your feelings say about your passions
5. What you can learn from past experiences
6. What you envision for yourself, (your dreams)
7. What your intuition tells you, and
8. How other people see you and what you can learn from this.

1. Twenty things you love to do

Take a pen and a piece of paper or use the action guide, and write down at least twenty things you love to do. They don't need to be related to a specific career or to be money-making activities. Just write down whatever you enjoy the most. These can be simple things such as going for a walk or listening to music.

Below is my list. Bear in mind it might be a little bit skewed since I really know what I love to do. I love:

1. Reading
2. Learning new things
3. Studying the human mind
4. Learning about the nature of reality
5. Helping people succeed
6. Helping people design their ideal life
7. Playing sports
8. Going for walks
9. Dancing
10. Talking about ways to change the world
11. Making a difference
12. Improving things
13. Having deep one-on-one conversations
14. Connecting with people at a deep level and finding out what their passion is
15. Making people laugh
16. Inspiring people
17. Writing
18. Learning foreign languages
19. Living in different countries and learn their culture, language and way of thinking, and
20. Observing people and animals

As you can see, many of the things on my list, such as reading, going for a walk or observing people and animals are not money-making activities, at least, they don't seem to be.

Now, for each activity on your list, write down the benefits and underlying value(s). There are no right or wrong answers. Just do your best. As you do so, see if you can find any patterns. For example, you may notice some values are expressed several times. These values could be freedom, security or a desire to connect with other people for instance.

Identifying the top five things you love the most

The purpose of this exercise is to start brainstorming potential career ideas based on the top five things you love the most. Don't hold back, welcome even the silliest ideas. Forget about the practicality of your ideas or even whether or not you have any interest in pursuing them. Just come up with as many ideas as you can. Because your perspective is limited, you might want to ask your family and friends to join you. You're likely to come up with more ideas this way.

Take a sheet of paper, write down in the middle, "Things I love the most" and draw a circle around it, (we'll do a lot of this throughout the book). Now create five branches and at the end of each branch add one of the things you love the most. For each item you love, jot down all the ways you could potentially make money out of it. Each idea represents a sub-branch. Dig deeper and look for potential jobs or careers that could be a good fit for you.

Let's say you love walking in the countryside. Now, how could you make money out of this activity? Here's a list a client of mine created, (reproduced with kind permission):

- Tour guide
- Photographer
- Travel agent, (she also loves traveling)
- Painter

Of course, this list is just a starting point. We can go much deeper. For each idea you had, ask yourself whether this is something you would enjoy doing. For instance, I love walking outdoors but the last thing I want is to become a tour guide. For activities you could potentially enjoy, dig as deep as you can. For instance, if you're interested in being a tour guide, ask yourself:

- Do I want to stay go overseas?
- If I want to work overseas where would I go?
- Who would be my clients?
- Would I do this full-time or part-time?
- What similar job might I enjoy doing?
- What aspect of being a tour guide particularly interests or excites me? What does this say about my personality, values, passion or strengths?
- Etc.

This exercise can help you identify some of your interests or passions and start connecting them with potential career ideas. Later, in the section "Five Lives," we'll see how you can further clarify your real passions and work out how to make a living out of them.

2. What you focus on and think about most often

What you spend time thinking about can give you some hints regarding your passions. If you're passionate about something, it isn't too much of a stretch to assume you would think about it often. Ask yourself the following questions:

- What do I daydream about most of the time?
- What do I think about before going to sleep or when I wake up?
- What do I think about when I take a shower, drive or commute to work?
- When I get bored, what do I think about?

Exercise - Jot down what you daydream about

For an entire week, take a couple of minutes in the evening to jot down what you thought about during the day. At the end of the week, read your list and see whether you can find any patterns. Are there common threads? If so, what can you learn from them?

3. What you like to do in your spare time

Now let's look at your actions and behaviors and see what you can learn from them in regard to your passion. The following questions will particularly help you.

A. What are you naturally drawn to do during your spare time?

For instance, my mother enjoys history. For fun, she reads countless of books and spends many hours doing genealogical research. If she really wanted to, she could have made a career out of her passion—and could still make money out of it today.

As for me, I'm curious about the power of the mind. I spend most of my free time reading books and trying to understand the nature of the mind and how reality works. Often, I'm so eager to learn that I can't sleep.

What about you? How do you use your spare time? What does it say about your interests and passions? Now, let's say you didn't have to work a day in your life, how would you spend all your free time?

B. What do you volunteer for?

Have you ever volunteered for something at work? Is there something you would like to volunteer for? Often, what we willingly and proactively seek to do is a strong indicator of our interests. What about outside of work? Do you support a certain association or perhaps volunteer at the school your children attend?

During my first job at a prefectural office in Japan, I created a newsletter in which I talked about the cultural differences between France and Japan. I didn't have to do it but found it really interesting. This initiative already showed my interest in both writing and human psychology. At the time, I had no idea I would end up writing books on personal development.

So, what do you volunteer for and what does this say about your passion? Could you do more of this activity at your current work or could you find another job that would allow you to spend more time doing similar activities?

4. What your feelings say about your passion

You can learn a lot by observing your emotions. As I wrote in my book *"How to Master Your Emotions,"* your emotions are here to guide you and, if you listen to them carefully enough, they will tell you what you need to know. While negative emotions signal your need to change something, feelings of joy, passion and excitement indicate that you're on the right path. The question you need to ask yourself is, how do I experience more of that joy and passion in my life? How can I design my life in such a way that I'm living to a purpose?

Let's look at some of your emotions and see how they can help you uncover your passions.

A. When was the last time you feel excited during a conversation?

Think of the last time you were excited. What were you talking about and what does it say about your passions? If you regularly find yourself getting excited about a specific topic it may reveal a passion worth exploring.

B. What are your interests? What would you like to learn more about?

I believe in the power of curiosity. In fact, I believe that curiosity is what allows people to become great at what they do. As

Einstein said, "I have no talent, I'm just passionately curious." I like how he uses both "passionately" and "curious." Once you discover what you're curious about and feel great passion for it, you're on the right path.

For instance, as I mentioned above, my mother is 'passionately curious' about history, while I'm 'passionately curious' about the power of the mind. I believe curiosity is the major driver for both my mother and me, but also for countless other people.

What about you? What do you want to learn? Foreign languages? History? Science? Gardening? Computer programming? Metaphysics? And why exactly is this?

What books, TV shows or documentaries are you naturally drawn towards? What does it say about your interests?

There are so many things you can learn and so many ways you can use these skills to design a fulfilling career. Take some time to reflect on what you're curious about and see how you can connect these things with specific jobs or careers. Be creative! Feel free to do the same exercise you did with the Five Things You Love Most.

C. Who do you envy, admire or feel jealous of?

Have you ever felt jealous of someone who seems to have the perfect life? Why is that? What does this person have you don't?

Please note, we are not talking about material possessions or physical appearance, but about what this person does for a living. Do you envy someone because he or she is doing exactly what you want to do? If so, what does it say about your passion?

To give you an example, I felt jealous of successful personal development bloggers because they were doing exactly what I wanted to do. In fact, this is how I got started with blogging. I thought, "This is it. This is what I want to do with my life. I want to get paid to study psychology and grow as a person, while helping others improve their lives."

This feeling of jealousy led me to discover what I really loved.

What about you? Who do you envy? And why? Is it because they have the career you dream of, and if so, what does this say about your passion?

D. What painful issues or challenges have you faced in your life?

The challenges you faced in your life often gives you meaning and can even turn into life purposes. Perhaps, you overcame shyness and now want to help other people who suffer from the same thing. Or perhaps someone in your family is struggling with drug addiction and you feel a strong need to help people in the same situation. Look at the struggles you or your relatives have experienced and see whether you have an interest in helping others with similar issues.

E. What makes you angry? What do you find outrageous?

Anger often indicates an underlying passion and desire to change the status quo. Perhaps, you're angry at the fact there are too many homeless people in our cities. Or you might find it unacceptable that people still die from starvation. Or maybe you want to fight for animal rights. Have a closer look at what makes you angry and you may find a cause worth spending your life fighting for.

F. What do you hate doing?

Sometimes, the first step to identifying what you love is by looking at what you hate. Perhaps, you hate working in an office. Or maybe, you hate sales. Take time to create a list of the things you hate doing. It may provide valuable insights and help you avoid spending the rest of your life doing things you hate.

G. What will you regret?

Imagine you were to die today, what would be your biggest regrets? What are some goals and dreams you wish you had pursued?

What would you do if you had only six months to live? To make it more real for you, look at a date exactly six months from now. Make this future date your last day on earth. How does it feel? What would you do if you could dedicate these six months to what you love most?

5. What you can learn from your past experiences

What happened to you in the past, especially during your childhood can provide valuable information regarding your passions and innate talents. The following questions will help you with this:

A. What did you enjoy doing when you were a kid?

What you were drawn to do when you were a child may indicate natural talents or field of interests. Did you spend time outside building things? Or did you spend time reading books or drawing?

When I was a kid, I spent a lot of time reading books—which I still do today. I was eager to learn and would study country flags or study the dictionary in the search for new words. What about you? What can you learn from your childhood? Are there any hints you may have missed?

Additional tip: if you can't remember much about your childhood, ask your parents what you enjoyed doing when you were young. You may be able to gather some interesting insights.

B. What past successes are you most proud of?

The things we're proud of and remember the most vividly are often things that mean a lot to us. We're proud of accomplishments that resonate with who we are. So, what are you the proudest of in your life? And what does this say about you?

6. What you envision for yourself (dreams)

Now, let's use your imagination to see what your ideal life would look like. Try answering the following questions:

A. What would you do if you had all the time and money in the world?

Too often, a lack of resources prevents people going after what they want. They have to pay the bills and save money for their child's education. Let's assume for a minute time and money aren't an issue. What would you like to spend your days doing? Hint: Don't answer lying on the beach drinking Piña Colada— we've already covered this. Would you create art? Write books? Create a small business? Help the local community? Study?

B. What would you do if you could not fail?

Imagine you could not fail and could have absolutely everything you've ever dreamt of. What would you do? What would this look like? For the sake of this exercise, remove any limitations and give yourself permission to unleash your creativity.

C. How do you want to express yourself to the world?

I believe we all have our own personal way to express ourselves to the world. Some want to entertain others and make them laugh so they can forget their problems for a little while—think of Jim Carrey. Other people love to teach and share their knowledge. Yet others want to take care of people and enter the medical/caring profession. Some means of expression are:

- Creating art

- Entertaining
- Healing
- Inspiring
- Inventing
- Managing
- Putting things together
- Taking care of people, and
- Teaching.

If you had to choose only one way to express yourself, what would it be?

Once you gain clarity regarding your means of expression, you'll find it easier to select the right career and new opportunities will open for you. For instance, perhaps, until now you were convinced you had to be a school teacher. However, by understanding what you love above all is teaching, you may now start exploring other teaching-related activities. It could be running educational programs in a commercial organization, teaching private courses or running workshops.

D. What do you want to be remembered for?

One day you will leave this planet. The question is, what do you want to be remembered for? In what way did your existence matter? How did you impact the world? What values do you want to embody? It doesn't have to be anything big, but you want your epitaph to be clear and unambiguous. So what footprint do you want to leave?

E. Writing your eulogy

Imagine you've just passed away. Your family and friends are attending your funeral. What are they saying about you? What would you *like* them to say about you?

The following exercises will help you identify the gap between who you are and who you want to be.

Exercise 1: Imagine what your family and friends would say about you if you were to die today.

Exercise 2: Write your own eulogy, (what you would like people to say about you). To do so, describe:

- Who you were as a person, (qualities and values). Mention your courage, willingness to help, kindness or whatever values you genuinely want to embody. Put it differently, write down what type of person you want to become.
- What you were about, (your mission and vision).
- How fulfilled you felt, (your fulfillment). Describe how happy you were as a result of living life with a purpose.
- What you've accomplished, (your impact on the world). Write down the impact your actions had on people. How did you make a difference in the world?

F. What do you want your (future) kids to do with their lives?

Sometimes, we project onto our kids the life we wish we had. What career do you have in mind for your kids? And what does it say about you and your interests?

Note that sometimes, we want our kids to have a certain career because of the social recognition that comes with it—doctors, lawyers etc. If this is the case, be honest with yourself, as this doesn't say much about your passion.

G. What are your family members making a career of or dreaming of?

Look at your relatives' current careers and dreams. What are they doing? What about their dreams? Can you find a common thread? Is there anything—career or dream—you would be interested in pursuing?

7. What does your intuition tells you

Listen to your inner voice. What does it tell you to do? To gain clarity, start asking yourself questions. A good time to do this is before going to sleep or right after waking up. This is when you have better access to your subconscious. You can ask question such as:

- What should I do?
- What career should I pursue?
- What do I really want?

Don't try to come up with an answer using your mind. Just let the question sink in while doing your best to empty your mind. Trust there is something within you that already knows what you're here to do.

8. How other people see you and what you can learn from this

A. What feedback do you receive from people?

What are your family, friends or colleagues complimenting you on? What do they think your strengths are?

B. What do your parents think you should be doing? Why?

What your parents want you to pursue as a career can provide you with valuable clues regarding your real passion. Even if you disagree with their choices, ask them why they think this way and see if there is anything you can learn from the information.

How trying more things can help you find your passion

Some people know intuitively what they love, while for others the discovery may take time. If you still don't know what you'd love to do with the rest of your life, I encourage you to try as many things as possible. Look at things that pique your curiosity and try them out.

It took me ten years to find out what I really wanted to do with my life. It doesn't mean these ten years were wasted though. During those ten years, I kept focusing on what I felt like doing at the time. After graduating high-school, I went on to study English and Japanese. English was one of the few subjects I really enjoyed, and I had started studying Japanese as a hobby. After I received my master's degree in Japanese Studies, I moved to Japan where I worked for a few years. Then, I entered a business school and join a consulting firm there. To say I wasn't passionate about my job is an understatement. As recently as 2014, I discovered my vocation was to study personal development and, if possible, make a living out of it. Shortly afterwards, I started my blog, and I soon became determined to leave my job to focus full-time on my passion. It was the only option I could think of pursuing.

The point is, it took me ages to find out what I wanted to do with my life. All the things I did to get where I am today, were stepping stones, giving me new skills and helping me clarify my purpose. I hope that by performing the exercises in this book, you'll save years of soul searching.

Now, am I saying once you find your passion everything will be easy, and you will be a big success? Absolutely, not. I also wrote this book to help you develop the mindset you need to make a living from your passion. I know whatever skills you need, you can develop. Whoever you need help from, you can contact. And, as you take one hundred percent responsibility for your life, develop self-discipline, and remain patient, you'll be well on your way to achieving the results you want.

So, keep trying new things. Keep searching. It may take you a few months, a few years or more to find out what you really want to do with your life, but that's fine. Perseverance is key.

Action step

Complete the exercise in the action guide (*Part 3. - Finding out what you love*).

9

CREATING A MISSION STATEMENT

Do you have a mission, or do you have a job? In this section, we'll discuss how to create a mission statement for your life.

A mission statement is simply a sentence that tells you what you're here to do.

Why a mission is more important than a job

Most people have a job. The problem with a job is that your identity often becomes tied up in it. People with a long-term career often struggle to find meaning in their lives after they retire, which is why you should have a mission not simply a job. What difference would it make to your life if you couldn't wait to wake up every day ready to work on your exciting mission?

How a mission differs from a job

A mission encompasses both your personal and your work life. It is significantly broader than a job and can be fulfilled in many different ways. Because of this, losing your job or retiring can never prevent you from living your mission. You will still be able to fulfill your mission by searching for another job, doing volunteer work or creating your own business.

The key is to align what you do with your mission. For example, my mission is to help people find their passion and achieve their goals, so they can become the best version of themselves and make their biggest contribution to the world. This is not just a job, and I can fulfill my mission in multiple ways. For instance, I can:

- Become a teacher
- Coach people
- Create programs
- Organize seminars, and/or
- Write books.

I'm sure there are many more ways to fulfill my mission. I know I will never stop learning so I can become better equipped to help people. If I 'fail' at one thing, I'll simply move on to the next. The only way I could be out of sync with my mission is to pursue the wrong career but, because my mission is clear, this is unlikely to happen.

Another key characteristic of a mission is you can't simply turn it on and off. While you can forget about your soul-crushing job at soon as you leave office—which is what I did with my previous job—your mission has no 'off' switch. It doesn't mean you have to be a workaholic and neglect your family. It simply means you don't need or want to forget your mission.

How much more likely are you to succeed by having a mission? When you have a mission, you go the extra mile. You constantly think of ways to help people. You're excited to take action and eager to learn. Your curiosity provides you with an incessant desire to learn and understand things. When you're in a state of curiosity, you start tapping into the power of your mind. Once you make the decision to continue learning, you build new connections in your brain and rewire it. As you keep learning, you will eventually become one of the most knowledgeable people in your field.

How to find your mission

Creating a specific and compelling mission statement can take time, so don't worry if you still lack clarity. Let's do a simple exercise to help you find your mission.

First step: Finding out how you want to express yourself and contribute to society.

One of the most effective ways to identify your mission is to define specifically your personal means of expression. Do you want to teach? Inspire? Entertain? Organize? Build? Invent? Touch people's hearts with your art? Support? Protect?

Another way to look at it is: how do you want people to feel as a result of your actions?

Find three verbs that resonate the most with you. Remember, these three verbs should reflect how you want to express yourself and/or how you want people to feel as the result of your actions. My three verbs are:

- Empower
- Inspire
- Teach

Second step: Identifying what you stand for.

Try to identify the one cause, principle or value that matters the most to you. Is it creativity? Excellence? Freedom? Joy? Faith? Justice? Passion? Compassion? Truth?

Third step: Clarifying whom you are here to help.

What group of people, organizations or causes do you want to support? Below are some more examples:

Groups of people.

- Children
- The Elderly
- Homeless people
- Battered women
- Drug addicts
- Alcoholics
- Researchers
- Inventors
- Entrepreneurs
- Stay-home moms, and
- Growth-oriented people.

Organizations:

- Government
- NPOs
- Small businesses
- Businesses in a specific industry
- Businesses in a specific country or region
- Business supporting a specific cause

Causes/Issues

- Women issues
- Cancer
- Environmental issues
- Animals rights
- Hunger
- Domestic violence
- Human trafficking

You may want to serve several groups or causes. In this case, either pick one, or to combine all of them into a bigger group. Note that the more specific you group, the better. As an example, when I did this exercise, I came up with the following: "growth-oriented people who want to fulfill their mission."

After completing this exercise, I came up with the following mission statement: "to empower, inspire and teach growth-oriented people to unlock their greatness and live on purpose."

Did you create your personal mission statement? How do you feel about it? Does it inspire you? When you read it, do you feel compelled to take action?

Additional tips:

Your mission statement is unique. You don't need to share it with your family or friends—unless you want to. Neither does it have to resonate with anybody but you. If it isn't as compelling as you would like it to be, refine it. If you are unable to refine it now, return to it later, but do it!

Action step

Complete the exercise in the action guide (*Part 3. - Creating a mission statement*)

10

CREATING A LONG-TERM VISION

Having a compelling vision is essential. As Helen Keller said, *"The most pathetic person in the world is someone who has sight but has no vision."*

A specific vision gives you a clear direction to follow. It allows you to stay focused on the results you want and to adjust your actions each time you deviate from your ultimate goal.

Successful people didn't get where they are by merely wishing it would happen. They became extremely clear about what they wanted, created a detailed plan of action, and spent most of their time, effort, focus and intent on turning their vision into reality.

Once you establish a long-term vision, you can start to align your daily actions with your long-term vision. Everything you do becomes a stepping stone toward your ideal vision.

Look at it this way, airplanes constantly correct their trajectories based on wind speed, direction and other factors. Because the destination is known in advance, all the necessary corrections can be made to ensure passengers arrive safely at their destination. This is how you should think of your vision. Your journey won't be a straight-line from A, where you are today, to B, where you want to be. Instead, you will make a series of monthly, weekly or even daily adjustments along the way. You may even encounter turbulences, U-turns or delays, but eventually, you'll reach your desired destination. Your ultimate destination depends on the following factors:

- Your core values, which influence all the decisions you make
- Your innate talent and strengths, which determine what you should focus on
- Your passion, which further determines where your energy will go, and
- Your mission, which encompasses all the above elements.

Now you know more about your personality, innate talents, values and passion, and have designed a mission statement, it is time to craft an exciting vision for your career and your life. I can guarantee having a specific and compelling vision will propel you ahead of most people merely living paycheck to paycheck with no clear vision for their future. You are the creator of your life, so start acting accordingly. Focus on what you want to create and use the infinite/astonishing/wondrous power of your mind to turn the invisible into the visible.

Imagine yourself ten years from today. Where are you? What are you doing? What does your career look like? Who have you become? What about other areas of your life? What contribution are you making to the world?

The main characteristics of a great vision

1. Specific

Your vision has to be specific. You must be able to visualize it with clarity. Ask yourself, how will I know I have achieved my vision?

What would your ideal day look like?

A great way to make it more specific is to envision what your ideal day would look like?

Morning

- What time will you wake?
- What will you do first thing in the morning?
- What will you be eating for breakfast?
- What will you be doing? Will you be working? If so, what exciting things will you be working on and with whom?

Lunch

- What will you eat for lunch?
- Will you eat out or at home? If you eat out, where will you eat?
- Who will you eat with?
- How long will your lunch break be?

Afternoon

- What will you be doing? Will you be working? If so, what exciting things will you be working on and with whom?
- For how long will you be working?
- What fun activities will you be doing?

Evening

- What will you be doing?

- Who will you spend your time with?
- What will you eat for dinner?
- Will you eat out or at home? If you eat out, ideally where will you eat?

Who do you want to become?

Another way to create a great vision is to think of the person you want to become. What skills and qualities will you have developed?

Skills

What skills do you need to master? Some examples are:

- Coaching skills
- Leadership skills
- Marketing skills
- Public speaking skills
- Sales skills
- Technical skills, (engineering, programming etc.)
- Writing skills

Qualities

What qualities do you want to develop? Some examples are:

- The ability to listen
- Assertiveness
- Concentration
- Confidence
- Generosity
- Patience
- Persistence
- Positivity
- Proactivity

- Reliability
- Self-awareness
- Self-discipline

2. Emotionally charged

Your vision should be inspiring. There should be emotionally strong reasons why this vision *must* become your reality. Your vision should:

A) *Reflect your values*

Your vision should be a means to express your deepest values and live by them as often as possible. For instance, if you want total freedom in your life, it should be reflected in your vision. If you want to spend as much time as possible with your family, this should also be something one can tell simply by looking at the ideal day you designed in the previous exercise.

B) *Reflect your personality*

Your vision should allow you to express your personality. If you're an introvert and want to spend a lot of time by yourself or in one-on-one conversations, your ideal day should have reflected this as well. If you consider yourself as a Maestro, your vision should indicate your desire to become a true master at whatever you're passionate about.

C) *Reflect your mission*

Your mission is how you want to express yourself to the world. Your vision is a physical manifestation of this mission through both inner changes—who you become—and outer changes—the impact you have.

Look at your mission statement. What inner and outer changes do you want to happen as a result of fully living your mission?

Remember, people tend to overestimate what they can

accomplish in six months while highly underestimating what they can do in ten years. If you act upon a crystal-clear vision, you can accomplish more in ten years than most people do in a lifetime.

Exercise - creating your long-term vision

Imagine yourself in ten years from now. Where are you? What does your career look like? How are you contributing to the world?

* * *

Action step

Complete the exercise in the action guide (*Part 3. - Creating a long-term vision*)

PART IV

WINNING THE INNER GAME

In the long run, people usually do achieve their goals if they persist, stay flexible, and don't give up. The biggest challenge for most people is persisting long enough to win the mental game.

— STEVE PAVLINA, PERSONAL DEVELOPMENT BLOGGER
AND AUTHOR.

Your mindset largely determines your ability to achieve your goals—whether they be career goals or not.

At the beginning of this book we laid the foundations when we discussed the importance of believing in yourself, taking one hundred percent responsibility and facing the truth. Now, let's go one step further.

To create a winning mindset and create your dream career, I believe you need to develop three key mindsets:

1. The *Asking Mindset*: Giving yourself permission to pursue

your goal and accepting you're worthy of it. With an *Asking Mindset* you broadcast your desire to the world and ask for what you want.

2. The *"I Can" Mindset*: Removing mental blocks and believing you *can* achieve your goals. With an *"I Can" Mindset*, you take action towards your goal with little to no inner resistance.

3. The *"I Will" Mindset*: Developing a long-term perspective and sticking to your goal until you achieve it. With an *"I Will" Mindset*, you move towards your goal with consistency and great patience until you attain the results you want.

In addition to these three key mindsets, you must also surround yourself with a team of people who fully support your efforts. We'll see this in the fourth and last part of this section when we discuss how to create an empowering environment.

11

THE BENEFITS OF AN ASKING MINDSET

When you adopt an *Asking Mindset,* you give yourself permission to work towards your goal. You accept you're worthy of it and, as a result, you feel confident sharing it and asking for support. This, in turn, creates situations to help you obtain what you want faster.

Sharing your goals

By sharing your goals, you:

- **Offer other people the chance to help you:** The more you share your goals, the more likely you are to encounter people who can help you achieve them. There are 7.5 billion people on this planet, and some of them have the resources you need to achieve your goal. But they can only help you if they know what you need. For that, you must tell them about your goals.
- **Make your goals real:** When you share your goals, they become more concrete. You start seeing yourself as the type of person who can actually achieve them,

which increases your self-confidence. In addition, it puts you in a position where you have to grow to match the new identity you're broadcasting to the world.

Asking for support

Failing to ask is one of the main reasons you don't get what you want. Because when you don't ask, the answer is always, "No." Did you know that, right now, by not asking, you're missing out on countless opportunities?

- Did you ask for a raise? Perhaps, if you do, you'll get it.
- The person you like, did you ask them out on a date? They might say "Yes."
- Did you ask your friends to help you find an apartment or a job? They may know someone who can help you.
- Did you ask if you could have lunch with the person who has your dream career? They might give you valuable advice.

Below are some more things you could ask for.

In your current job

- A raise
- A promotion
- Flexible hours—e.g. working from home once a week, etc.
- Holidays
- Developing an exciting project that could benefit your company
- Changing your job description
- Changing jobs within your company
- Having lunch with a colleague/boss that could help you make a positive change in your career

Related to your future career

- Recommendation letter/testimonials
- Contacts from people who could help you develop your career
- Advice from people who have the exact career you want
- Scholarship/grants/loans
- Free/paid internship in a field of interest to you

These are just a few examples. I'm curious. Have you asked any of these things? Remember, to design a fulfilling career you must be proactive and go after what you want. Do so and you're more likely to get what you want in the long run.

How to develop an Asking Mindset

Here are a number of practical tips to develop an *Asking Mindset*. I've divided the section into the following parts:

1. Preparing mentally before asking
2. Activating the receiving process
3. Doing the actual asking

1. Preparing mentally before asking

In this section, we'll see how to remove some of the fears that may prevent you from asking for what you want.

a) *What is the worst thing that can happen?*

What if they say no? What if they hate me for being pushy? What if they think I'm selfish? What if they don't want to talk to me anymore and we lose our friendship? These may be some of the fears that are running in your mind right now.

Before you ask someone for help answer this question, "What is the worst thing that can happen?" Let's say you want to send a message to someone to ask if they would like a free copy of your new book. What is the worst-case scenario in this situation? Perhaps, they will reply, saying they read your book and absolutely hated it. They might even leave you a one-star review on Amazon and suggest you stop writing. Or they may ignore your message. Now, how likely is it to happen?

b) *Is this more important than my dream?*

Now, even if some of the scenarios mentioned above were to happen, would it be such a big deal? What do you think is more important: Your dream of making a living doing what you love or one of the scenarios mentioned above? Let me give you two more tips to help you remove/overcome the fear of asking.

a. *Remember you're going to die*

In Ancient Greece, Stoic philosophers use a technique called negative visualization. They would visualize losing important things in their lives to better appreciate what they already have. They would imagine losing their loved ones or their house and meditate on their own death.

While thinking of your own death may sound depressing, it can also be empowering. Remembering you're already naked, to paraphrase Steve Jobs, allows you to overcome fears and take more action toward your dreams. You're going to die, so while you're alive, why not live to the fullest? Most of the things you need to ask to achieve your goals aren't such a big deal, but if you don't ask for what you want, you'll be filled with regrets as you grow older.

b. *Realize people love to help*

Have you ever felt good as a result of helping someone out? While you may be reluctant to ask for help, the fact is that many people *love* to help. They like to contribute to other people's success and make a difference in others' lives. When you seek their advice, people feel valued, which makes them feel good about themselves. So, don't be shy. Let people help you. By allowing people to help you, you make them feel good while strengthening your relationship. It's a win-win situation.

2. Activating the receiving process

Now, let's discuss how you can facilitate the receiving process and make it easier for you to both ask and receive.

a) *Asking the subconscious*

Have you ever come up with great ideas after a nap or while taking a shower? It is said that Thomas Edison would take cat naps when looking for answers to challenging problems. He would often wake up with the answer he was looking for. Sometimes, when we try too hard to find answers, our minds erect barriers. In some cases, simply by letting go and allowing our minds to relax the answer can be revealed to us—almost magically.

To develop this aspect of your 'asking' mentality, ask your subconscious for support. One way to do so is by asking yourself questions you want an answer for before going to bed or taking a nap. Your subconscious is your biggest asset so why not ask for its help?

See this exercise as another tool in your toolkit. Every tool that can move you closer to your dreams is worth using, isn't it?

b) *Giving unconditionally*

Learn to give more of what you want to receive. The more you give the more you open yourself to receiving. While, it may sound mystical, it isn't. By giving what you want to receive, at the subconscious level you allow yourself to receive that very same thing. It becomes natural to you. And the more natural something feels, the more likely you are to attract it.

Unfortunately, most people think of giving and receiving as an exchange between two persons/people. I believe this is a subpar approach. With such a mindset, you generally expect people to reciprocate when you help them, which makes the giving and receiving process more constraining.

Another way to see this process is as a relationship between you and the entire universe. You help as many people as you can without expecting anything in return. Then, you receive. People you help will likely reciprocate, but it's not essential and this is perfectly okay if they don't. Similarly, you may reciprocate when people help you, but if you can't, that's fine as well.

You might think it's selfish not to reciprocate to a kindness but think of it this way. Isn't it selfish to help someone but then expect them to reciprocate? Wouldn't you feel better if you could help people without expecting anything in return? And, if people could do the same for you, wouldn't it be less constraining and more natural?

c) *Accepting you don't need to know everything*

Have you ever felt you should know how to do something, but you don't? In the past, this type of thinking has caused me a lot of trouble and prevented me from asking for support when I most needed to.

Let me give you an example to illustrate my point. When I was a consultant, one of my first projects involved taking charge of updating a financial simulation. There was one problem though: my spreadsheet skills were almost inexistent. That was despite the fact I had already worked for four years and earned an MBA. How could this be? Was I that stupid? The fact is, my previous job didn't require me to work with spreadsheets. When I started my MBA, I was so ashamed of my lack of knowledge,

I relied mostly on other people's skills, learning just enough to avoid getting into trouble. This skills gap made me feel as though I wasn't good enough and, because I was afraid everybody would discover how stupid I was, I avoided asking for help until one day I couldn't hide anymore. I faced the truth and asked for help and, guess what? It didn't kill me. I could have avoided so much stress if I had been willing to face the truth and ask for help when needed. This has been a recurrent pattern in my life and has manifested in many different ways.

Don't assume you should know something. Accept the fact you can't know everything. Accept reality and be willing to ask for help.

3. Doing the asking

Now, let's see concretely how to ask for what you want.

a) *Making it a habit to ask for what you want*

Most of us have been conditioned not to ask for what we want. But with enough practice you can turn asking into a habit, like anything else. Why not develop the habit? To begin with, start with small requests. This will help you reclaim your right ask. Below are some examples of small requests.

- Ask for water at the restaurant.
- Ask if you can borrow someone's pen.
- Ask to have a look at something.
- Ask for a free sample of something.

The idea is to get in touch with your feelings and, instead of censuring yourself, to give yourself permission to ask for what you want. We often refrain from asking because we don't think our needs are important or fear being rejected or disturbing people. However, by holding back, we tell our subconscious mind our preferences don't matter.

Here is the truth: Your preferences *matter!* It is okay to get what you want, so why not ask? Who knows what could happen? As the Bible says, "Ask and you shall receive."

If you were bold enough to ask for it right now, what one thing would make the biggest difference in your life?

b) *Practicing outside-of-the-box asking*

Once you're used to asking for small things, you can further develop your *Asking Mindset*, by asking for more than you expect to obtain. Too often, people make assumptions regarding what they can and cannot ask. This is one of these "assumptions about life." By doing so, they limit their thinking within the narrow range of what they deem reasonable. They're afraid to break rules. However, rules aren't set in stone. In fact, you *can* ask for whatever you want. It doesn't mean you'll receive it, but there's nothing stopping you from asking, right?

When you stretch yourself and ask for more, you'll find out that some people will go the extra mile to support you. Their actions, in turn, will start chain reactions that could lead to positive results. Remember, if you don't ask, the answer is always no.

What would be a good example of asking for whatever you want? Well, perhaps you know someone who is living your dreams. You could ask them to be your mentor. Alternatively, you could ask them questions such as, "What would I need to do to be in your position?" Or "What programs would you recommend?" Make sure you share your dreams and what you've done to achieve them so far. The more you can demonstrate how serious you are, the likelier you are to receive a positive answer.

Another great example would be to ask people around you if they know someone who could help attain your goals.

Remember, most people are willing to help, especially if they share the same passion.

Learn to ask for more. Regularly ask yourself,

- How can I ask for more? What crazy thing would allow me to make progress faster if I only decided to ask?
- Who could help me the most if I were to help them first?

Try to think outside of the box. Keep asking and you will be well on your way to getting what you want.

c) *Asking the right questions*

As Tony Robbins says, "*quality questions create a quality life. Successful people ask better questions, and as a result, they get better answers.*" Instead of asking vague questions, ask questions that reflect what you really want. If you want to be the best coach you can possibly become, don't ask coaches how to become a coach. Ask them questions such as, "What would I need to do to be one of the best coach in the world? What books or programs can/will help me get there? What training do I need to undertake? What skills do I need to master? Who do I need to meet? What would I need to believe? If you were in my shoes, what would you do?" Etc.

The four obstacles preventing you from asking

Have you noticed how reluctant you are to ask for help? What makes it so challenging to ask for what you want? I believe they are four main reasons for this:

1. Fear of rejection
2. Fear of disturbing people
3. Fear of not being good enough
4. Pride

1. Fear of rejection

Being rejected is one of the things people fear the most. It is related to the way our brain is designed to ensure survival. In the past, being rejected by our tribe or peer group, deprived us of access to key resources such as food or protection, which could lead to our death. Rejection would also jeopardize our chances to reproduce and pass on our genes. It's no wonder we try so hard to fit in.

Nowadays, being rejected by a person or a group is generally not such a big deal. It's certainly not life-threatening and bears little to no consequences. When you ask, people *will* sometimes say no, but remember, if you don't ask the answer is always no anyway, so you might as well give it a shot.

2. Fear of disturbing people

Another reason we are reluctant to ask is the fear of bothering people. We assume they probably have better things to do with their time. And who are we to ask them for help? Why not reframe the situation by realizing people generally *love* to help others?

3. Fear of not being good enough

Sometimes, we are afraid of people's reaction to our request. Perhaps, we want them to give us feedback on our product, book, essay or video and we fear what they may say. However, the only way to become better and achieve our goal is to face the truth head-on, reflect on our 'failures' and improve continuously. Hiding our heads in the sand will only slow our progress.

Adopting a long-term perspective can helped us manage feelings of inadequacy. I've found the two following mantras particularly useful:

- I can always learn, I can always grow, I can always improve.
- I have time.

Try them for yourself or create similar mantras of your own.

4. Pride

Do you want to do things on your own, refusing any help? The idea you can do it alone is a myth. No one ever does. To create the life you want, you'll need the help of others. That's the truth. The sooner you realize it the better off you will be. I have to admit, I find it challenging to ask for help. However, even as a writer who seemingly works alone, I need help. I couldn't do what I do without my designer or my editor. If not for Amazon, I wouldn't have a platform to sell my books. If I didn't have fellow writers to offer advice and help promote my work I would be struggling. Not to mention my readers and subscribers, without whom I would have no audience.

You need help from other people to get what you want. Swallow your pride and ask for all the help you need.

* * *

Action step

Complete the exercise in the action guide (*Part 4. - Developing an Asking Mindset*).

12

DEVELOPING AN "I CAN" MINDSET

With the *"I Can" Mindset* you remove mental blocks and limiting beliefs to help you move freely towards your career goal. You overcome limiting beliefs, fear and self-doubt and clarify your goals to ensure nothing can prevent you taking action.

The truth is, whatever your goal, there are specific reasons why you haven't been pursuing it wholeheartedly. Unless you uncover these specific reasons, you'll continue struggling to achieving your goal(s). These reasons are:

- **Limiting beliefs:** You hold disempowering beliefs. Perhaps, you believe your too old, too young or not smart enough, which prevents you from going after your goal.
- **Fear:** Because you're afraid to fail, you postpone your goal to a nebulous point in the future rather than setting a clear deadline. Having a specific timeframe for your goal would make it real and you're uncomfortable with that.
- **Lack of clarity:** Your goal is too vague, and/or you

struggle to define a specific plan of action to reach it. Or you're unsure whether you want it or not. As a result, you're unable to commit one hundred percent.

- **Self-doubt:** You're genuinely excited about your goal, but you don't believe you can actually achieve it, perhaps due to the fact that you have failed to achieve similar goals in the past.

Mental blocks can—and need to—be removed if you are to design the life you genuinely want.

Limiting beliefs

The first step is to ask yourself why you haven't already achieved your goal. Your completely honest answer is likely to be an excuse or limiting belief, for example:

- I'm not ready yet.
- I'm too old to change career.
- My job isn't that bad after all.
- There is just too much competition.
- Well, I didn't really have time because [***add the spurious reason here].
- What are my parents/spouse/friends going to think?

I invite you to take a pen and piece of paper and write down your honest answers to the above question. Now, have a serious look at all your answers and ask yourself:

- Is this really true? Is there absolutely nothing I can do about this?
- If I were one hundred percent committed, what would I do? What would it look like?

- Am I really too old to change career?

- If I were absolutely committed to changing career, what would I do? What specific actions would I take?

- Is there really too much competition?
- If I were one hundred percent committed to taking a piece of the pie in my field of choice, what would I do?

- Do I really not have time to dedicate to my dreams every day?
- If I were really committed, how could I find the time to work on my goals every day?

- Should my parents/spouse/friends decide what should my life be?
- Is that true? If I were one hundred percent committed what would I do to work around that issue? How would I convince them? What would/could I do?

Fears

The second step is to look at your fears. Have you set a deadline for your goals? If not, why not? What are you afraid of? Are you going to postpone your dream to some distant future—probably never? How would that make you feel as you lie on your deathbed? Would you regret not having pursued your goals? Would you feel like an idiot for not having taken the first step toward your most important goal?

So, what are you afraid of? Failure? Success? Perhaps you are scared people will laugh at you if you fail?

Whatever the case may be, you have to be honest with yourself and face your fears. You are probably making them bigger than they actually are. After all, our brain is afraid of the unknown, which is why we often prefer to stay in our comfort zone rather than chase our dreams. It is safer that way.

But is this how you want to live?

Lack of clarity

Do you know exactly what you want? Oftentimes, we can't move forward because we lack clarity. We want something but we're unsure what that is. Or we don't know whether we actually want it. This lack of clarity can prevent us committing one hundred percent to our goals. I've noticed that when I struggle to commit to my goal it is usually for three main reasons:

1. They aren't clear enough, and I'm unsure of what to do —a clarity issue.
2. They are clear, but I don't know how to achieve them— a strategic issue.
3. I'm not sure they are really what I want, and I feel some resistance—a passion issue

Do any of these issues prevent you committing to your goal? If so, make sure you spend time to resolve these issues, so you can remove any resistance and fully commit to taking action toward your goal. The exercises in this book will help you gain clarity, create a specific action plan and uncover your passions.

Self-doubt

Do you genuinely believe you can achieve your career goal? If not, why is that?

Another reason you may have difficulties committing to your goal is simply because it isn't realistic, which prevents you from committing to it wholeheartedly. How do you feel about your career goal? On a scale from 1 to 10 (where 10 is high and 1 is low), how confident are you that you will achieve it within the timeframe you set? If your answer is anything below 7 you might find it necessary to redesign your goal. You can do this in two ways. Either by setting a more realistic goal or by extending the original deadline. As Jack Canfield says, there aren't and unrealistic goals, only unrealistic timeframes. Even your wildest goals may be possible if you give yourself enough time to achieve them.

Your goal may also seem out of reach because you haven't broken it down. For instance, a one-year goal of losing thirty pounds in excess bodyweight might sound totally unrealistic but once you break it down into monthly and weekly goals, you may feel reasonably confidence of success. That would mean losing on average 2.5 pounds per month or a little over half a pound per week. Doable, right?

Eventually, only you know what is realistic for you. What sounds impossible right now could be realistic in a year from now as you develop more self-discipline and when success boosts your self-esteem. The better you become at achieving your goals—even small ones—the more confident you'll be in your ability to tackle bigger goals.

Once you get these four factors right—overcoming limiting beliefs, removing your fears, clarifying your goal and making them realistic—you'll find it much easier to commit one hundred percent to making it happen.

Now, let's see how you can overcome limiting beliefs in greater detail.

Overcoming limiting beliefs

Limiting beliefs are the main reason why most people never achieve even a fraction of their capabilities. In reality, you have an incredible ability to grow and evolve. You can overcome procrastination, enhance your self-discipline and remove most of your fears. You can also develop the habits you need to get from where you are to where you want to be. This includes the habits of:

- Taking one hundred percent responsibility for your life
- Setting daily goals and achieving them
- Asking yourself the right questions
- Being self-compassionate
- Being intentional about everything you do
- And many more.

By becoming the best person possible, you open yourself to new opportunities. Goals that previously seemed impossible are suddenly within your reach.

We've already discussed what's preventing you from achieving your career or life goals. We also started questioning some of your beliefs by asking whether they were true. The next step is to disprove these beliefs by looking at real life counterexamples. While you may be busy looking for excuses to avoid changing your career, other people are changing despite their personal limitations.

Look at the disempowering story you're telling yourself. Let's say you believe you don't have enough time to invest into your career goal. Can you find people in similar situations who successfully managed to change their career? We all have 24 hours each day and, if other busy people can do it, so can you.

Or perhaps, you believe you're too old to change your career, and you may even be reminded of that 'fact' by your family and friends. Again, look for people who have achieved their goals despite their "advanced age." The best place to start is by looking online. The examples below will start loosening the belief you're too old:

- Fauna Singh ran a marathon when she was more than one hundred years of age.
- Anna Mary Robertson 'Grandma' Moses didn't start painting until she was 76. In 2006, one of her paintings sold for $1.2 million.
- Nola Ochs, Model Richardson, and Leo Plass earned their college degrees at ninety-five, ninety and ninety-nine, respectively. Nola started writing her first book, Nola Remembers, when she was one hundred years old.
- Helen Klein started running when she was fifty-five. She ended up completing more than sixty marathons and one hundred and forty ultra marathons.
- Julia Child wrote her first cookbook at aged fifty and became a celebrity chef.
- Colonel Sanders was sixty-two when he first franchised Kentucky Fried Chicken in 1952.

If all these people were able to achieve their goals despite their age, so can you. Of course, there are limitations. You're not going to become an NBA player if you're forty years old and have never played basketball before. However, if you're determined enough, in many cases, age will not prevent you from achieving your career goal.

I invite you to search out case studies relevant to your career goal. Write them down in your action guide or in a dedicated journal. Look for people who were in the same situation as you—lack of time, lack of resources, no formal education and so on—but still managed to change their career.

Visualize the consequences

Select one limiting belief. Ideally, the one you feel is holding you back the most. Now, use the Stoic method and visualize the consequences of clinging to that belief. If you don't change anything, what would be the long-term consequence? Perhaps, you'll have to stay at the same dead-end job until you retire. If so, feel the pain. How will it impact your health? Your happiness? Your energy levels? Your relationships within your family? What regrets will you have on your deathbed? We are motivated by both pain and pleasure. Let your pain motivate you to **make** the changes you want to experience in your life.

Writing down your new belief

Now you have identified the limiting beliefs holding you back, write down your new belief. Ask yourself, "What new empowering belief(s) could replace my old limiting belief(s)?"

Let's look at some concrete examples:

- I don't have time —> I make the time for whatever is important to me.
- I'm too old —> Age is just a number. Other people have achieved similar goal, and so will I!
- There is too much competition —> I'm fully committed to achieve my goal. Competition is irrelevant.

Your turn now. Write down your new empowering belief(s).

Turning your new belief into an affirmation

Now you have decided on your new belief, turn it into an affirmation. Affirmations are statements you tell yourself—or write down—again and again until you believe them.

Turning your new belief into a positive affirmation will allow you to focus on what you want while ignoring what you don't want.

Repeating your affirmation multiple times throughout the day will turn it into a belief, which will affect your thoughts and actions. Below is some advice on how to create a powerful positive affirmation:

1. **Use the first person:** Start your affirmation with "I."

2. **Use the present tense:** You want your belief to be something you are embodying now. This is why it's important to use the present tense. You can use "I am" to emphasis the fact that it is part of your identity or "I am -ing" to condition your mind to believe it is already happening. Some examples would be:

- I am committed to making the time for whatever matters to me.
- I always make time for things that are important to me.

3. **Avoid negation:** Never use "don't" or "not." Remember, it's better to focus on what you want to become than on what you want to move away from. Here are examples:

- Good example: I'm young and fully committed to creating my dream career.
- Poor example: I'm not too old to change career and I will not give up.

4. **Make it short:** The shorter the affirmations, the easier they are to say, and the more impact they tend to have.

- Good example: I make time to do whatever I'm committed to do.
- Poor example: I do whatever I can to find the time because I'm truly committed to designing the career I've always dreamed of.

5. **Ensure you resonate with the affirmation at an emotional level:** Rather than saying something mechanically,

come up with an expression that touches you at a deep level. A good way to start is to write down any quote or expression you love as a source of inspiration.

6. **Visualize:** As you repeat your affirmation, visualize the ideal outcome and feel it. What does it feel like to be committed to achieving your goals? Remember, visualizing isn't the same as daydreaming. When you daydream, you *wish* that one day you'll achieve your dream. When you visualize, you *commit* to making it a reality. Try to feel the difference.

7. **Engage your body:** To make it more effective, use your body. As the famous coach Tony Robbins says, to change your emotions state you must change your physiology. That's why he has been practicing incantation—not affirmation—for several decades. See his video here to get a sense of what incantations are.

8. **Believe in it:** Avoid doubting yourself. You have the right to accept the/your new belief. Take notice whenever you start doubting your new belief and, when this happens, focus on your affirmation. Tell yourself you can always discard that belief at the end of the initial thirty days. During the allotted thirty days, do your best to remove self-doubt and learn to believe in yourself.

If you follow the above guidelines, you should be able to come up with an effective affirmation and implement the belief(s) needed to achieve your goal.

I encourage you to set a few minutes aside every morning—or every night—to repeat your affirmations. You can use the if … then method to do so. With the if … then method, you set specific conditions as triggers to certain actions. Below are some examples of how you can use this method:

- If I wake up, then I repeat my affirmation for five minutes.

- If I'm taking a shower, then I repeat my affirmation.
- If I go to the bathroom, then I repeat my affirmation.
- If I walk from my car to my office, then I repeat my affirmation.

It's your turn now. How can you introduce an if … then condition in your daily schedule to ensure that you repeat your affirmation?

Action step

Complete the exercise in the action guide (*Part 4. - Developing an "I Can" Mindset*).

13

DEVELOPING AN 'I WILL' MINDSET

One of the reasons people fail to achieve their goals is because they give up too soon. This is due to several factors:

- They misjudge the amount of time and effort needed to achieve their goals.
- They underestimate the power of perseverance.
- They focus too much on the results rather than the process.

Adopting an *'I Will' Mindset* means you develop a long-term perspective and fully understand the power of patience. As a result, you avoid common traps and manage to remain motivated long-term until you finally achieve your career goal.

1. Misjudging the amount of time and effort needed

In general, people are terrible at planning. They tend to be overly optimistic regarding what they can accomplish short-term, while underestimating what they can accomplish long-term. As a consequence, they are prone to giving up before reaping the fruits of their efforts. As an example, here is what happened to Grant Cardone when he quit his job to create his own business:

> *I assumed it would take three or four months to get back to that income level of the job I previously had. Well, it took me almost three years to get my business to provide me with the same amount of income of my previous job. That was twelve times longer than I had expected. And I almost quit three months into my new business venture. Not because of the money, but because of the amount of resistance and disappointment I was experiencing.*
>
> — GRANT CARDONE, AUTHOR AND SALES TRAINING EXPERT.

What about you? Have you ever misjudged the amount of time and effort needed to achieve your goals? Is it possible you gave up too soon? And what would you do to avoid repeating the same mistake?

2. Underestimating the power of perseverance

People tend to give too much importance to external factors such as talent or luck, failing to realize that with enough effort and persistence their goals are possible. They underestimate what they are truly capable of doing and forget the most important thing: they can always learn, grow and improve. As a result of this underestimation, they become impatient when they don't achieve their goals. Or, worse, they stop improving, believing they've reached their limits. This is seldom the case. More often than not, their approach is the problem. By putting in place a different type of practice and reflecting on their performance weekly or even daily, they will improve.

3. Overly focusing on the results

By learning to focus on the process—what you do every day—rather than on the results—the target you set—you will dramatically increase the chance of achieving your goals in the long run.

For instance, let's say you want to lose weight. A result goal would be to lose twenty pounds by the end of the year. A process goal would be to eat a certain type of food and to exercise on a consistent basis. There is no guarantee you will lose twenty pounds, but if you follow the process every day, over the long term you will generate good results and will likely achieve your goals—even if it takes more time than you thought.

Once you commit to changing your career, be willing to spend a few years until you end up exactly where you want to be. That's a normal process. Every successful individual knows it requires tons of effort and a lot of patience to make significant changes in one's life. Do not give up before you reach your target. Hang in on there.

Give yourself enough time to change your career. Set a clear deadline, two to three years from now, (this may take longer depending on how challenging your career goal happens to be). Then, make a promise to yourself you will never quit before this deadline. If you do so, you'll be astonished by what you can accomplish in just a few years.

If you wish to learn more about how to achieve challenging goals, I encourage you to check my book, *The One Goal*.

Action step

Complete the exercise in the action guide (*Part 4. - Developing an "I Will" Mindset*).

14

DESIGNING AN EMPOWERING
ENVIRONMENT

Wouldn't it be nice to be in an environment that inspires you to be the best you can be every day? To design an empowering environment, it is essential for you to:

1. Surround yourself with positive people who will uplift you.
2. Expose yourself to inspirational content.
3. Set powerful habits that will improve your mood long-term.

1. Surround yourself with positive people who will uplift you

As entrepreneur, Jim Rohn said, "*We are the average of the five people we spend the most time with.*"

Who are these five people for you? Do they encourage you to strive to reach the maximum of your potential? Or are they telling you to be 'realistic'and to forget about your goals and dreams?

You often live up to people's expectations. When people expect the best from you, you're compelled to learn, grow and improve. You stretch yourself and, as a result, achieve more than you would have ever imagined. On the other hand, when people discourage you from pursuing your dreams, you tend to stay in your comfort zone.

Do you know what the self-help "gurus," Jim Rohn, Tony Robbins and Jack Canfield have in common? They all have (or had) great mentors. Jim Rohn was penniless until he met his mentor Earl Shoaff. Tony Robbins worked for Jim Rohn when he was a teenager, and Jack Canfield's was mentored by W. Clement Stone, the publisher of *Success Magazine*. Do you think they would have been so successful without their mentors? Possibly, but having a mentor must have helped, right?

The bottom line is, when it comes to designing your ideal career and life, it matters who you hang out with. Therefore, you should strive to surround yourself with:

1. People who lift you up, and
2. People who have what you want and know how to get it.

And if you can't, the Internet is your friend. On it, you'll find videos, articles and programs from the best people in your field. What's more, the information is often available free or is very inexpensive. You're also one click away from millions of books that could change your life.

Getting rid of negative people

First of all, let's see how you can remove negative people from your life—or at least reduce their negative influence on you so you can design a more empowering environment. Below are four things you can do:

A. Cut negative people from your life: Sometimes, people around you can be so negative you have to make a radical decision: Stop seeing them. The question to ask yourself is, "Is this person seriously hampering my chances to achieve my goals and dreams?" If the answer is a clear "yes," you might have to make a difficult decision.

B. Reduce the time you spend with negative people: It's not always easy to remove people from your life. Sure, you can cut ties with some of your friends, but what about your family members? Are you going to stop seeing your mother or father because they don't support your choices? That's a tough call. Sometimes, the best thing is simply to spend less time with negative people. Perhaps, you can choose to see your negative family members or friends once in a while instead of regularly.

C. Share your dreams and goals strategically: Another thing you can do is avoid talking about your goals in the presence of negative people. When the only thing you're likely to get from sharing your goals is a good laugh or a sarcastic comment, keep them to yourself.

D. Get support from negative people: Finally, whenever possible, try to generate support from negative relatives/friends. Let them know how much their support means to you and show them your level of commitment. At first, you may not receive the encouragement you want, but as you start gaining small wins, people around you will realize how serious you are. When the time is right, tell them you need their support.

2. Expose yourself to inspirational content

To create an empowering environment, you must condition your mind every day and focus on what you want as often as possible. You might do this by reading inspirational books in the morning or in the evening before going to bed. Or it might be by consuming content related to the career you want to design. As a matter of fact, to succeed long-term in making a living doing what you love, you must be willing to learn every day until you become a subject matter expert in your area(s) of interest. After all, when you genuinely love something, you naturally want to study it and become better at it, don't you?

For instance, if you want to become a full-time writer, write and learn how to become a better writer every day, and meticulously study the topics you're writing about.

If you want to become a coach, read books on coaching, interact with other coaches and practice coaching as much as you can.

How many people tell you how one day they will open a restaurant, a bar or a cafe, but haven't even taken the first step to doing so? How many talk about their dreams of becoming a freelancer, a coach or a real estate investor, but haven't read a single book or take a single course on the subject? Don't be like them! Strive to become the best you possibly can. Don't leave it to luck. Take one hundred percent responsibility and resolve to make it happen.

Finding role models

Who is your role model? Who are you jealous of because they have the career you desire? Identify at least one person who has exactly what you want and learn everything you can from them. Consider the following questions:

- How did they get there?

- What blueprint did they use and how can you replicate it? What are some of the key milestones on the road to reaching your goal?

- Who do they know?

- What does their network look like and how did they create it? Specifically, what can you do to create a similar network long-term?

- What challenges did they overcome?

- What barrier—self-defeating behavior, lack of resources, absence of network, physical disability, lack of education —did they overcome and how?

- How do they think?

- What is their mindset and what new empowering belief must you adopt to obtain similar results?

- What do they do on a consistent basis?

- What is their daily routine? What do they do first thing in the morning? What powerful habits do they perform every day and how can you implement similar habits in your life?

In short, what gaps do you need to fill in?

- What do you need to work on to obtain similar results? Do you need to work on your confidence, learn new skills, implement new powerful habits, network with people, let go of limiting beliefs or change your environment?

So, who are your role models and what can you learn from them?

Now you're armed with the mindset needed to achieve your goal and have designed and redesigned your environment, let's see how you can identify the right career for you and create a clear plan of action to make it happen.

For further reading on how to develop a great mindset and step up your game in all the areas of your life, refer to my book *Upgrade Yourself: Simple Strategies to Transform Your Mindset, Improve Your Habits, and Change Your Life.*

3. Set powerful habits that will improve your mood long-term

Sadly, many people are in a reactive mode. They go through life never decided exactly what they want. They prefer to have dreams or fantasies instead of going after what they want wholeheartedly. They're afraid that if they don't achieve their goals, they'll feel like a failure. Doing nothing becomes their default option. Their lack of proactivity is apparent the very first second they wake up, as they hit the snooze button of their alarm clock. When they finally manage to get out of bed, they go through their usual routine mindlessly. They don't set clear intentions for the day. They don't write down what they plan to accomplish and when.

To design an empowering environment, you must take control of your day. You must clarify what you need to do and plan your day, week, month and year to the best of your ability. This habit alone will go a long way to helping you achieve your goals and dreams. You must also have daily habits or rituals that allow you to start you day on a positive note. A productive day often starts with a productive morning routine. Reading inspiring books and working on exciting projects first thing in the morning will build momentum. You'll feel good about yourself and be inspired to accomplish even more. Working on your most important task first thing in the morning—or *eating that frog*, as Brian Tracy wrote in his best-selling book *"Eat That Frog"*—is also an effective way to boost your productivity.

So, what two or three habits, if performed every day, would help you achieve your goals in the long-term? Is it reading books in your field of interest? Contacting certain people? Setting daily goals? Don't overestimate the power of habits. The impact of daily routines—even simple habits—compounds over time and can lead to exceptional results in the long-term.

* * *

Action step

Complete the exercise in the action guide (*Part 4. - Designing an Empowering Environment*).

PART V

SETTING THE IDEAL GOAL

15

FINDING THE ESSENCE OF YOUR GOAL

One of the common traps when setting goals is being overly attached to a specific goal. While being determined to achieve a goal is powerful, sometimes it can lead you to feel discouraged and frustrated when this goal seems out of reach.

This attachment comes from the belief that only one goal can satisfy you. However, this is seldom the case. Your purpose is generally much broader than that. A specific goal is merely one way to fulfill your purpose.

For instance, let's assume your dream is to become an NBA coach. This is certainly not an easy path. Now, what could be the essence of your goal here? Is it being a coach? If so, would being the coach of a high-school basketball team be as satisfying a goal for you? What about another sport like baseball or soccer? Would that work? Or is basketball a must? If so, would working as staff for a basketball team work? What about being a commentator, writing a basketball blog or opening a store that sells basketball jerseys?

To help you find the *essence* of your goal, look at the mission statement you previously created. If you remember, my mission statement was:

Empower, inspire and teach growth-oriented people to unlock their greatness.

Based on this mission statement alone, I can already start figuring out some potential careers. Perhaps, I could coach people. Or I could organize personal development seminars. Maybe I could become a counselor to help people figure out their ideal career. I could also write personal development books.

By knowing the essence of your goal, you can start narrowing down your choice of careers. And that's exactly what we want to do. At the same time, notice how the essence of your goal fails to take into account many other factors such as your strengths, talents, personality, core values or whether you're an introvert or an extrovert.

In the previous example, my mission statement doesn't say whether I want to spend my days teaching people or writing inspirational books alone in the comfort of my home. It doesn't say much about my strengths either—though my strong interest in helping people reach their potential could suggest I'm naturally good at it, which may or may not be true, (I'll let you be the judge of this). As you now understand, there are many possibilities depending on the essence of the goal.

What about you? What is the essence of your goal?

Below is a list of questions to help you clarify the essence of your goal further:

- Could your goal—or a similar goal—be viable in a totally different industry? If so, how would you feel about it?

- What are the core values behind your goal? Could other goals allow you to express these core values in a similar way?

- How do you express yourself through this goal? Do you

entertain people? Educate them? Heal them? Build something or invent something new?

- Could you come up with different goals that would allow you to express yourself in similar ways? (For instance, giving private courses to students or teaching English to employees instead of teaching English in High-school)

- If you could achieve only part of your goal, what would be the minimum you'd be satisfied with? Why? Think in terms of:

- **Money:** What if your salary was only half of what you want?
- **Location:** What if you have to live in the countryside rather than in a big city or vice-versa? In a different part of the world? In a smaller house/apartment?
- **Work environment**: What if you could do the same job but had to sit in front of a desk rather than at home or be self-employed? What if you had to work in a team rather than alone?
- **Time spent on your goal:** What if you could only work on your goal part-time(For instance, a writer who could write only for twenty percent of your time)
- **Working hours:** What if you had to work longer hours? Would you accept that job? And how many hours per week would you be willing to work?
- **Schedule:** Would you be willing to work late at night or weekends?

What did you learn about your career goal by answering this series of questions? How did the answers help you extract the essence of your goal?

Now, try to articulate the essence of your goal in as few words as possible. As an exercise, write down three to five different versions of your career goal while doing your best to keep the essence of it. As a reminder, your career goals are specific expressions of your mission statement. They may be particular jobs for instance.

This exercise will help you realize you have much more flexibility than you believe when setting goals. It will also allow you to check whether your original goal is right for you. If you need to revise your goal now, do so. Remember, goals are here to improve your life. Keep tweaking your career goal until you find what resonates with you the most.

* * *

Action step

Complete the exercise in the action guide (*Part 5. - Finding the essence of your goal*).

16

IDENTIFYING THE EMOTIONAL CORE BEHIND YOUR GOAL

Now, let's have a look at the emotions behind your goal. See the emotional core as the second layer that goes on top of the first layer, the essence of your goal. Your emotional core consists of the values you care about. By embedding values in your career goal—or any other goals—you energize your goal, which gives you the motivation you need to achieve it. Too often, people set goals without having a strong emotional connection to them. No wonder they have such a hard time motivating themselves.

So, what is the emotional core behind your goal? What will your goal bring you? How does it make you feel? Why is it important to you?

Let's have a closer look at what your goal will give you. Why is this goal important to you? How will it change your life once you achieve it? For instance, let's assume you want to create an online business. Why is this important? Is it just to make money or is there something more? If it's just for the money, you'll probably give up when you fail to obtain the results you want quickly enough. If you have strong emotional reasons, however, you'll persevere during tough times.

Now, let's say you want to create an online business because you want to:

- Be independent and having no boss to tell you what you do (autonomy)
- Be able to visit your parents more often, (family)
- Spend more time with your wife and kids, (family)
- Spend time doing what you love, (passion)
- Take longer vacations, (freedom, family, passion)
- Travel around the world, (freedom), and
- Work on your own, (autonomy, alignment with your introversion).

Close your eyes and imagine all the benefits of achieving your goal. How would it make you feel if you could spend more time with your family? What about being your own boss? Traveling around the world? Feels pretty good doesn't it?

Now, which goal do you think will energize you the most? The original goal of making more money or the emotionally charged one? In both cases the goal remains the same, creating an online business, but the 'why' behind it changes everything, doesn't it?

Let's say you also want to make more money. If so, don't stay at the surface. Go deeper by asking yourself what money will do for you. Below is a list of possible examples:

- Being able to buy healthier and more expensive food, (health)
- Buying a home closer to your parents, (family value)
- Investing into a passion project, (passion)
- Providing your children with a great education, (family value)
- The ability to retire early and do what you love, (freedom/passion), and
- Traveling/taking longer vacations, (freedom/passion).

The more emotionally charged reasons you can come up with, the more motivated you will be. Now, let me share with you my emotional reasons for making more money:

- Being able to buy the healthiest food I can find
- Being able to receive all the training I want and attend personal development seminars from world-class experts
- Having more money to give to charity and more time to serve other people
- Not having to worry about money anymore, and
- "Retiring" early and spending the rest of my life doing what I love, (writing, reading, traveling, learning foreign languages etc.).

As you now understand, your goals are all about emotions and values and are connected to your personality, strengths and passion. You pursue a certain goal because it makes you feel a specific way *and* is aligned with who you are. Once you set the right goal for you, you'll naturally be pulled toward it. You won't have to push so hard to achieve it. That's why it's essential for you to identify what you really want.

Now that you've identified the essence of your goal, take a few minutes to write down all the benefits of achieving it. The best way to do this is by creating a spider diagram. Take a sheet of paper and write the essence of your goal in the middle. Draw a circle around it and create separate branches to represent each a different benefit. Do your best to come up with as many emotionally charged reasons as possible. When he noticed the/a lack of motivation to accomplish a goal, Stefan Pylarinos from ProjectLifeMastery.com, likes to come up with a hundred 'whys.' He then selects the most inspiring reasons. What about you? How many reasons can you think of?

Action step

Complete the exercise in the action guide (*Part 5. - Identifying the emotional core behind your goal*).

17

ENERGIZING YOUR GOALS

By now, you should have a list of emotional values attached to your career goal. If not, returned to the previous section repeat the exercise.

Let's go one step further by looking at each emotional benefit in greater detail. Take your list and for each benefit and ask yourself the following questions:

1) What exactly would this look like?

2) Why does this matter?

Try to answer each question in as much detail as possible. The more specific you are, the more emotional fuel you'll receive. Let's look at our previous examples of building an online business.

Spend more time with your wife and your kids (family)

What exactly will that look like?

- I will enjoy a slow breakfast with my wife/husband and my kids each morning.

- I will go to every one of my son's soccer games.
- I will spend quality time with my wife each night.

Why does this matter?

I want to be here for my family. I don't want to miss key moments with my children due to work commitments.

Travel the world (freedom)

- I will travel abroad with my family for an entire month each summer. We would visit exotic places enjoying fun activities together and sharing moments we will remember for the rest of our lives.

Why does this matter?

I want to travel more with my family and knowing that I can do so whenever I feel like it is important for me, (assuming it's a school holiday or that you home school your kids). It gives me a sense of freedom that makes me feel as though I'm in control of my life.

Work on your own (autonomy, alignment with your introversion if relevant)

- I will avoid the stress of the rush hour commute and work from the comfort of my home.
- I will be able to set my own schedule and fully enjoy time with my kids in the morning, rather than rushing to work.
- I will be able to spend most of my time alone in a quiet environment of my choice, (assuming you're an introvert and this is what you want)

Why does that matter?

I love the feeling of being in charge of my life. Independence is important for me.

These are just a few examples. Now, look at your list of benefits and for each of them dig deeper. Produce a vivid picture of what each benefit will look like. Then, go deeper and ask yourself why it is so important for you. Remember, the more specific, the better.

* * *

Action step

Complete the exercise in the action guide (*Part 5. -Energizing your goal*).

18

INTEGRATING YOUR GOAL INTO YOUR LIFE

The next step is to make your goal part of your life. Do you often complain because you have insufficient time left to do what you love? Well, you will have to find the time. When you're serious about your goal, you will make the time for whatever you're committed to.

The best way to make a living doing what you love is simply by starting to do what you love. How else could you do it? Perhaps, you have a busy schedule and believe you cannot find the time. If this is the case, start small. Dedicate five or ten minutes to your goal each day. Over time you will build momentum and will naturally want to do more of the same. You'll find creative ways to free your time and dedicate more time to your goal.

There are several ways to work on your goal. I believe the best approach is to dedicate time to it first thing in the morning. Learn to prioritize. Whatever's most important to you, do it first. Otherwise, as the day gets busy, you risk forgetting about it and lose momentum.

At the beginning of each week block chunks of time to focus on your goal. Make sure you schedule them in a calendar or a notebook. If you can't work on your goal first thing in the morning, do it as soon as you finish work and/or during the weekend. You can also use your lunch break.

I recommend you dedicate between thirty minutes and one hour daily. This schedule will ensure you make progress towards your goal and maintain momentum. Of course, you can spend more time if you'd like to and are able. You can spend your entire weekend working towards your goal. Remember, the more time you spend on your career goal, the faster you'll see results.

Five Lives

In their excellent book, *Wishcraft: How to Get What You Really Want,* Barbara Sher and Annie Gottlieb provide the reader with a great exercise to help identify their passions. Here's the exercise:

Imagine that you had five lives, what would you do in each life?

The truth is that no matter how dedicated you are to a specific cause or mission, you probably have several passions. Unfortunately, you cannot dedicate time to each of them, or not to the extent you'd like to. The *Five Lives* exercise will help you identify your passions and integrate them into your life. You may choose to make a living from one or more of them while you keep other lives as hobbies or postpone them.

So, if you had five lives, what would you do? Perhaps, if you could start over, you would become a singer in this life and a teacher in the next. In yet another life, you could be an adventurer traveling the world, learning foreign languages and publishing books to share your story.

My five lives are:

Life #1 - The traveler

In this life I am a traveler living in various countries around the world while learning the language and discovering the local cultures. I've done a little of this in the past and plan to do more of in the future.

Life #2 - The researcher

In this life I am a researcher studying the human mind, both theoretically, by reading countless books, and practically, by going to personal development seminars, retreats and workshops. This is more or less what I'm doing now.

Life #3 - The actor

In this life I am an actor playing in B series or commercials.

Life #4 - The elite athlete

In this life I am an elite athlete. Perhaps, a road cycle racer, a marathon runner, a tennis/table tennis player or a martial arts expert.

Life #5 - The businessman

In this life I am a successful businessman in a field I love

Okay, it's your turn. By now, you should have:

- Identified twenty things you love to do and, among them, five things you *really* love to do
- Brainstormed potential career ideas based on these five things, and
- Clarified the essence of your career goal.

Using your previous answers, try to determine what you would do if you had five lives. Imagine you could do anything you wanted. Let your imagination run wild. What would you do?

Once you've identified your five lives, the fun begins. You'll probably notice that at least one of your lives includes elements from the ideal career you want to create.

In my case, *Life #2 (The researcher)* is more or less what I'm doing now. I'm still missing parts of it, such as going to various seminars or retreats, but I plan to do these things in the near future.

I did a little bit of *Life #1 (The traveler)*, as I lived in Japan for many years and learned to speak the language. I also plan to travel in the future and learn more foreign languages such as Spanish, Portuguese, Italian or Thai.

Life #3 (The actor) is something I would be interested in doing. I remember how much fun it was to create videos in Japanese— one of our assignments when I was studying Japanese. However, I would consider this as a hobby rather than a career.

I love sports as I enjoy testing the limits of my body and my mind. Being an elite athlete would allow me to do just that. Unfortunately, my joints hurt, and I can't practice much sport these days. That's why, I'll have to be reborn to live *Life #4 (The athlete)* to the fullest.

I would be interested in being a small business owner perhaps. I also like (healthy) competition and enjoy working with others toward a common goal I care about. At the same time, I like being free and independent, so perhaps *Life #5 (The businessman)* will have to happen in another life.

The point of this exercise is not to hope you'll be reincarnated enough times to experience five entire lives. It is to see whether you can have a taste of each of them while you're alive.

Look at each of your imaginary lives. Can you think of ways you could start integrating at least some of them into your life? Doing so would allow you to further energize your goal and make it even more compelling. Below are some ways you can make them part of your life:

- **Identify the most important lives for you right now.** While some of your five lives may be very important to you right now, others may not have a high priority. For example, studying the human mind (*Life#2*) is important to me but being an actor (*Life #4*) isn't really. Which life is the most important to you right now?
- **Combine different lives.** You may be able to combine some elements of the different lives. For instance, I could study the human mind by reading books and going to seminar while living in different countries and learning foreign languages (*Lives #1 and #2*). Perhaps, I could even create a company and hire people to help me out, (*Life #5*)
- **Live your lives simultaneously.** For instance, you could have a full-time job you love while playing in a rock band during the weekend. In my case, I could be studying the human mind and writing books during the week while recording videos with friends for fun. Of course, over the long-term it is also possible to turn one of your lives into a full-time job.
- **Alternate between lives.** For instance, I could spend three months in South America and learn Spanish (*Life #1*) while spending the remaining of the year studying and writing books (*Life #2*).
- **Live lives one after the other.** For instance, I could decide to study and write books for five years (*Life #2*) and then create a successful business (*Life #4*).
- **Promote/demote lives.** For instance, I could study and write books (*Life #2*) and create a business during the weekend. Then, as my business grows, I could go full-time with it.
- There are many different ways to play with your five

lives. Of course, you can also look at your lives and extract the essence of each of them. This will help you redesign them which will allow you to:

- **Identify ways to live them fully**. For instance, the essence of *Life #1*—traveling around the world—is to discover other cultures and learn foreign languages. Obviously, nobody is going to pay me just to travel and learn languages. I may, however, find other ways to live the same life. Perhaps, I can find a job that allows me to live in different countries around the world as an expat or work from anywhere in the world. It will depend on my other goals as well.

- **Redefine the goal.** For instance, it's highly unlikely I'll ever be an elite athlete in this life. Now, what is the essence of this goal? I believe it is my love for competition (with myself and others). Do I need to be an elite athlete to challenge myself? Of course, not. I can challenge myself in many different ways. Perhaps, I can set challenging goals that are more mental than physical. Or maybe I can identify a physical activity that is gentler on my joints. If I want to compete with others I can also try contests that don't involve sports. What about you? How can you redefine your goal, so you can still achieve the same benefits?

- **Come up with more realistic "lives."** Your ideal lives may require resources you don't currently have (time, money, network etc.). For instance, let's say I want to travel for three months to Portugal to learn Portuguese. If I currently have a 9-5 job, it's unlikely I'll be able to take three-month vacations, even if I call them sabbaticals. I will also require some savings. Perhaps, I can scale down the goal and go to Portugal for one week. I could study Portuguese in the mornings and go sightseeing in the afternoons. Before going, I could spend a few hours per week learning Portuguese, find Portuguese friends and/or watch documentaries about Portugal. Again, it depends on what the essence of my *Life #1* is. Discovering different culture? Sightseeing? Learning languages?

It's up to you how you want to live your "lives." You may feel strongly about one life. Or you may want to taste all of them to the best of your abilities.

For now, I would encourage you to focus on only one or two main goals (lives). If you're unsatisfied with your current job, pursuing the new career should be your main goal.

* * *

Action step

Complete the exercise in the action guide (*Part 5. - Integrating your goal in your life*).

19

SHIFTING YOUR IDENTITY

The truth is that if you already identified with the person you'd be when you achieve your goal, you would get there very, very quickly. The action would just flow.

— STEVE PAVLINA, PERSONAL DEVELOPMENT
BLOGGER AND AUTHOR.

How do some people achieve their goals while others fail? Is it through hard work? Well, hard work can't be the only answer. Otherwise, hard-working people would all reach their goals. To answer this question let's consider the following example:

Imagine you are currently overweight and want to lose 50 pounds. You've been struggling to lose weight for years. Now, put yourself in the shoes of someone with the 'ideal weight' such as a personal trainer. Imagine you—as a personal trainer—wake up one day carrying an extra 50-pounds of unwanted weight. How would you react?

You would be shocked. You would think, "This is not who I am. This is not acceptable," and you would instantly start transforming your body. You would remove all junk food from your house and exercise daily until you returned to your ideal weight. And you would do it as fast as possible. It would still be hard, but you would do it regardless. This is inevitable.

Now, why is it inevitable? It's because you have a specific image of what your body *should* look like and a specific idea of your health. This image is so closely linked to your identity, and you would inevitably return to your original weight. The only unknown is how much time it would take.

Money is another good example. Have you ever seen multi-millionaires losing all their money and make it back, seemingly in a heartbeat? Why is that? It's because they have a multi-millionaire identity. Sure, their list of contacts can definitely help, but that's not the main reason they make their fortune back. The real reason is that they consistently think, behave and act like multi-millionaires. They perceive money in a different way from the rest of us and, while $20,000 feels like a lot of money for most people, for them it's no big deal. As a result, they are comfortable negotiating huge deals or borrowing large sums of money while most of us would feel extremely uncomfortable doing so. The difference in mindset goes far beyond their perception of money, however. Their relationship with failure, the way they interact with people, and how they think is also different from the majority. It is no wonder that even when bankrupt, they behave differently from another person in the same financial situation. This is inevitable.

This example leads to the following question:

What if reaching your goal isn't so much about going from point A to point B, but more about shifting from Identity A—who you are—to Identity B—who you need to become to achieve your goal?

I believe both approaches are interconnected. By taking the

necessary actions to move from point A to point B, you become a new person. And by shifting your identity and focusing your effort on becoming a different person, you support the actions needed to move to point B.

Exercise - shifting your identity

Think of your career goal. What shift in identity would need to happen for you to achieve your goal? How would you be a different person?

The first step to shifting your identity is to think of what Steve Pavlina called the "side effects" of having achieved your goal. Put it differently, what would be different about your life once you've achieved your goal?

- What would be your core beliefs about yourself and about the world?
- How would you think differently?
- How would you feel?
- What would you do differently?
- What new habits would you have?
- What old habits would you have rejected?

If you're unsure of the side-effect of your career goal. Talk to someone who has achieved your goal and ask them:

- What would I need to believe to be in your position?
- What habits would I need to develop?

To achieve your goal, your beliefs and actions must match those of people who have achieved this goal. Now, it won't happen overnight. The key is to start closing the gap by progressively shifting your identity over time.

For instance, let's say my goal is to be a successful non-fiction writer. What would be the side-effects?

- I would write every single day like most successful writers do.
- I would introduce myself as a writer without feeling embarrassed.
- I would contact other successful writers like me.
- I would expect to sell a lot of books.
- I would find it normal to be invited to speak at events or even on TV or radio.
- I would expect to be paid a lot of money to speak at events.

It's your turn now. Take a pen and a sheet of paper and write down your career goal in the middle and draw a circle around it. Then, create the following branches:

1. Core beliefs, (who I am).
2. Feelings.
3. Actions/behaviors.

Add to each branch all the side effects of having already achieved your goal.

Action step

Complete the exercise in the action guide (*Part 5. - Shifting your identity*).

Creating your goal statement

Imagine you have achieved your goals and now live the perfect life, being successful at what you most love doing. How would you introduce yourself to someone asking you what you do for a living? Your answer to that question is what I call your "goal statement."

Would you lack confidence? No. You would merely state who you already are and what you are already doing successfully. Now, I would like you to write down your own goal statement with the following scenario in mind: You are attending an event, and someone asks you, "What do you do for a living?" What is your answer?

Visualize yourself as being already successful at your dream job. See yourself confident, energized and proud of what you do and who you've become. Now, write down your goal statement.

Once you've written your goal statement, put it somewhere you can see it and read it every day in the morning and in the evening. Rehearse out loud how you would introduce yourself to someone at an event. Engage your emotions. As you do so, cultivate a feeling of confidence, certainty and excitement. Keep thinking of your goal throughout the day. From now on it is who you are.

Action step

Complete the exercise in the action guide (*Part 5. -Creating your goal statement*)

PART VI

IDENTIFYING ALL THE RESOURCES YOU NEED

Do you lack the resources to get from where you are to where you want to be? In this section, we'll see what you can do about it.

As the famous life coach Tony Robbins says, *"It's not the lack of resources, it's your lack of resourcefulness that stops you."* You are a creator and no matter where you are right now, you have the power to transform your life. Once you take one hundred percent responsibility, find what you love and resolve to make it happen, you can find the resources you need to reach your goal whether it is time, contacts, money or mental support.

Let's identify the specific resources you need to make your dream a reality. Once you know what you need, you'll be able to start looking for ways to attract these resources.

Here are the different types of resources you may need to achieve your career goal:

- **People**: this can be people who can help you or people who can help find these people.
- **Information**: anything you need to know to maximize your chances of reaching your goal.
- **Finance/materials**: money or materials you need to achieve your goal.
- **Time**: additional time or ways to save time so you can focus on designing your career as fast as possible.

By having access to the right people and the proper information and having enough money and time, you can achieve almost anything.

Now, it's your turn. Can you identify exactly the resources you need to design your ideal career? Do you need more time, money or information? Do you need to meet the 'right' people? Or perhaps, you need more support from your family and friends. What will it look like to have all you need? Ask yourself, "If I could wave a magic wand and have access to all the resources I need to design my career, what would it look like?"

Now you have identified everything you need to design your ideal career, let's look at how you can access these resources.

20

FINDING THE RIGHT PEOPLE

Your personal network

Who do you need to meet? What meaningful relationships would help you achieve your career goal the most?

If you can't meet these people directly, who could help you connect with them? Start with what you have: your personal network. You already have a network of friends, colleagues and acquaintances, make sure you use it before looking elsewhere.

For instance, perhaps, you have a friend who knows someone who could help you. Or maybe he or she knows someone who knows someone who could help you. This is often how it starts. Often, what seem like weak connections can actually turn into valuable leads.

Exercise: Make a list of all the people who could potentially help you. This includes:

- People who have helped you in the past

- People you helped in the past (and who may feel 'obligated' to help you)
- People with potential connections in the field you want to work
- People with a certain influence and/or a big network, and
- People who could finance you or who know people who may offer financial support.

Reaching out to people

We now live in the world where we are just one click away from almost anybody else on this planet, and there are more than 7.5 billion people. Take the time to identify those who could help you achieve your dream. Consider the following questions:

Who are the right people for you?

Who are the key people who, if you were to meet, would help you most achieve your career goal? Before you even start reaching out, make sure you're actually contacting the right people. A few things to consider are:

- Do they have the power to make a decision? Can they actually hire you or introduce you to someone who could do so? Can they help you design your ideal career, and if so, in what way exactly?
- Do they have the resources you need or know people who have? Can they provide you with the financial support or the information you need to achieve your career goal?
- Can they boost your motivation in some way? Can they motivate you to raise your standards, provide you with valuable advice or keep your accountable? For instance, joining a group of authors has helped me raise my standard and stay motivated.

Where are they hanging out?

Where can you find them offline and online? Can you meet them at networking events? Can you interview them? Work for them? Contact them via social media?

What is the best way to contact them?

- Can you find someone who could introduce you to them? Do you have a friend or an acquaintance who could introduce you to the right person? Remember, being introduced to someone is way more effective than just sending an unsolicited email.
- If nobody can introduce you to the right person, what's the most effective way to contact them? Are they more likely to answer emails or is it better to send them a letter or meet them face-to-face?

How can you help them?

What do you bring to the table? Why should they offer you their support? What's in it for them?

Unless you put yourself in their shoes and understand what they value the most, you won't be able to network effectively with them.

Let's say you want to connect with the top people in your chosen industry. They must receive hundreds of emails every day from people who want something from them. If you were in their shoes, how would you feel? Would you want to help these people? What kind of emails would you reply to?

I believe there are several types of messages busy people are likely to reply to:

1. Messages they receive value from because you:

- Give a solution to a problem they have
- Introduce a perceived win-win situation, or
- Offer free help or advice.

2. Messages they can relate to because you:

- Show you understand what matters the most to them
- Know someone they know and trust
- Share a story they can relate to, and
- Remind them of their younger self when they were in the same position as you are now.

Now, let's do an exercise. Put yourself in the shoes of the top person in your chosen field of interest. What kind of email you would actually read and even reply to? Remember, you receive over three-hundred emails daily. Brainstorm some ideas. Think of how you could provide them value and/or how you could relate to them in some way. If you have a specific person in mind, go ahead and try sending them an email.

Offering value upfront

I believe the best way to network is constantly to offer value. For instance, if you want to connect with key players you could:

- Volunteer to work for free
- Offer solutions to make them even more successful, and
- Introduce them to other people who could help them— assuming you know such people.

Becoming the person they would help

Perhaps, you don't believe you have anything of value to offer (yet). That's fine. This may take time. Meanwhile, a key question to reflect on is, "What can I do to become the type of person they would help?"

Remember, most successful people are not cold. They just can't help everybody. In fact, they are partly in the position they are today thanks to mentors and other supporters. They understand the value of networking. Now, who do you think they are willing to help? People lacking commitment or people who demonstrate serious commitment?

The best way to become a 'serious' person is to take consistent action toward your goal, learn everything you can about your field of interest and improve your skills to the best of your ability. You want influential people to perceive you as being on your way to success.

Avoid wasting time waiting for that one person who will change your life. Instead, be in constant motion. Take action and never stop learning. Start gaining small wins. Have something to show for your work. Action and results speak louder than words.

Big fish vs. small fish

You may have tried to connect with big fish in the past without much success. Sometimes, you're just not yet in a position to connect with key influencers. If so, start with smaller fish.

Building a network of people who can help you is essential and small fish in your network could grow to become big fish in a few years. When this happens, you'll be in the position to ask for their support.

Being in the personal development field, I wish I could connect with "gurus" such as Tony Robbins or Brian Tracy. However, even if I did manage to grab their attention, it is unlikely they would do more than perhaps share one of my articles, which would have little to no impact on my career. Does it mean I shouldn't try to connect with key influencers? Of course, not. It just means I shouldn't rely on this method alone to achieve my career goals. I also need to create meaningful connections with other bloggers and writers in my field. This will allow me to:

- Access valuable information and advice from other people in my field, (networking allowed me to join an awesome group of writers on Facebook, and helped me find a great designer, a great editor and others, all of whom helped me raise my standards), and
- Offer opportunities for cross-promotion, (by connecting with other bloggers and writers I was able to promote my books to their readers and receive extra exposure).

I also encourage you to look for rising stars in your industry. If you spot people who are doing great work and have loads of potential, reach out to them and offer your help. They might not be able to reciprocate right away, but they may do so in a few years.

Additional tip:

Your networking strategy will also depend on the nature of your career goal. For certain jobs or careers, connecting with people with decision-making power might be critical, while for other jobs or careers, building a network of people you can collaborate with might be a more effective strategy.

Eight simple networking tips

Below are eight tips to help you network more effectively.

1. Don't do what everybody else does

Successful people received loads of emails. They can't read them all. They must decide which ones to read based on their subject lines. Over time, they learn to recognize recurrent patterns such as people (selfishly) asking for help or wanting to do business with them. Thus, if you do like everyone else, they will dismiss your email as spam.

Make sure you stand out. Again, put yourself in their shoes. If you received a similar email how likely are you to reply?

2. Choose the right channel

Emails aren't always the best way to reach people. Meeting them face-to-face or being introduced via a mutual friend is a far more powerful method. If you know their address, postal (snail) mail can also be an interesting alternative, especially if you send a handwritten letter or a simple (and original) gift. Usually, the more time and effort you put in, the better. Successful people are willing to do things other people don't, and so should you.

Don't forget to use Facebook and other social media platforms. While many people focus on increasing their followers, I believe the power of Facebook lies in the fantastic opportunity it offers to message people individually. Instead of counting your followers, start seeing Facebook as a massive online networking 'event,' and use it to reach out to people on a one-on-one basis.

3. Do your homework

Look for commonalities. Do you have similar hobbies, enjoy the same food or read the same books? The more specific you can be, the better. If you can teach them something or offer them valuable tips or information regarding a hobby they just started, it's even better.

4. Be specific

Avoid sending generic messages. Instead, make sure you craft a well-thought personalized message. If you mentioned something you like about their work, give specific examples. For instance, if they wrote an article you enjoyed, don't just say you love it; describe what exactly you love about the article and why. How did it impact your life? How does it relate to your own experience?

5. Get to the point

Make sure your message is succinct and clear. Don't hide your agenda. Busy people need to know your intention and what you expect from them. The shorter the message, the likelier they are to reply.

Make it easy for them to respond. To do so, avoid asking complicated questions. Limit yourself to one simple thoughtful question and avoid asking any questions you can easily find answer for.

6. Think long-term

Rather than trying to get something from people, think longer-term. For instance, start by letting them know you would like to connect with them in the future. Ask them if there is anything you can help them with. Better still, let them know *how* you could help them. When you want to make new friends, you don't try to get something out of them, do you? Why would networking be any different? Networking is a long-term game. The purpose of the approach is to build long-term relationships. Keep this in mind when you contact people.

7. Be authentic

Avoid manipulating people. Be authentic and interact with people you want to network with as you would do with friends. Don't use clever marketing techniques or hide your agenda.

8. Be patient

Creating personal and professional relationships takes time. Often, you won't get any response. Keep planting seeds for long-term relationships using the tips mentioned above and, over time, you'll build great relationships.

Action step

Complete the exercise in the action guide (*Part 6. - Finding the right people*).

21

FINDING MONEY

Let's be real. Giving up on your dream career while you haven't done anything in your power to finance it is not a valid reason, it's an excuse. Any obstacle, be it a lack of money, time or connections has one purpose: to test you. The truth is, you can *always* find reasons to abandon your goals. If it's not a lack of money, it's a lack of time, energy, skills or knowledge or it's because there is too much competition or because you're too young or too old. You name it. Whatever you can use to avoid facing your fears, you will. Money is often the most convenient and tangible 'excuse' available.

I'm not denying the fact you may not have enough money right now, I just want to challenge you a little and make you feel uncomfortable. I want you to identify the real reason for not pursuing your goal. How much is due to a lack money and how much is fear of moving beyond your comfort zone. Be honest with yourself, how big a part does fear play in your decision-making?

The first step to finding the money you need is to see through your limiting belief.

1. Fact vs. belief

Once you've acknowledged the part your fears play in preventing you from pursuing your goal, the second step is to ask yourself whether or not being able to finance your dream is a fact or a belief. Ask yourself:

- Is that really true I can't finance my dream? Is there absolutely nothing I can do about this?
- If I were one hundred percent committed to find the money needed to finance my dream, what would I do? What would it look like? What could it look like?

2. Degree vs. results

Before you start looking for ways to raise money remember the following: people don't pay for your degree, they pay for the results you get from them. They pay for the emotional impact you have on their lives. This could be by saving them time or money, making their lives easier, helping them lose weight or providing them with a product they love.

So, what's key for the specific career you want to create: earning a degree or getting your clients results? This is an important question to ask before investing thousands of dollars to gain a degree.

I'm not saying degrees are useless, I'm just saying they may not be essential for you. If they aren't and you can't afford them, find a workaround. Instead, focus on becoming the best you can be at what you do and constantly look for ways to improve. Nowadays, no matter what skills you need to develop, you can learn it online or in books without great expense. Continuous improvement and self-reflection will put you far ahead of people who stopped learning after acquiring their degree.

There are tons of jobs you can do without a degree. For instance, I've been telling my mother she should become an interior designer. She told me she would have loved to. My answer was, what's stopping you? She probably has another twenty to thirty years to live and plenty of time to do it. Not only that, but she's already creating boxes and redesigning old furniture that people love. She was unimpressed by the work interior designers did in her friends' houses, and I suggested she could start her new career by offering to redesign her friends' houses for free to gain experience and references. Again, people want to see results. If people saw her work and loved it, do you think they'd care whether she has a degree?

Before choosing to pursue a degree or investing in your education, make sure it is the best option for you. Obviously, for certain professions, a degree is essential, (lawyers, doctors etc.), and there is no way around. If so, you must find a way to finance your dreams.

3. How much money do you really need?

Sometimes, you may overestimate the amount of money required to start your venture or to acquire the skills you need. It is always a good idea to sit down and work out your finances first. Write down how much money you need to pursue your dream. Doing this alone will make the dream more concrete. It might even make you feel a little bit uncomfortable or scared, but this is a good thing.

4. Starting for free

Let me further challenge you now. Can you start without any money? Ask yourself the following question:

If you had no money at all and had no choice but to succeed, what would you do? What could you do? For instance:

- Could you start building your portfolio by providing free services? Maybe you can give free consulting, free coaching, take pictures for free or help people with their interior design as a way to gain more experience. Experience is one of your most valuable assets. While you might have great excuses for not studying for a degree, you have no excuses for not gaining the experience.
- Could you volunteer to help someone in the position you aspire to be? If so, do you have specific skills you could use to help him or her? For instance, perhaps you can help with marketing to boost their sales. Or you may simply help them with administrative tasks to get a foot in the door.
- Could you develop skills the people with your dream career lack? By doing so, you could help them and become an insider.
- Could you focus only on what requires little to no money such as developing valuable skills online or connecting with people in the industry? At the same time, you can start saving/making more money to finance your dream.

5. Reevaluating the essence of your goal

Before you try to obtain money, it is also important you have a closer look at your career goal. What is the essence of your goal? What are you really trying to attain/gain? For instance:

- Could you achieve your career goal without having to borrow money?
- Could you start with non-financial aspects of your goal? For instance, perhaps you can start developing some valuable skills by reading books or watching videos online.

- Could you reframe your goal, so you need less money to achieve it?
- Could you think of similar, more affordable careers?
- Could you identify less expensive career paths that would act as effective stepping stones toward your end goal?

6. Obtaining financial support

Who said you have to use your own money to finance your dream? If you don't have the money, it's faster to use someone else's money instead. The question is: who could finance you? Below is a list of a few ways you can find the money you need:

- Donations/crowdfunding
- Grants/Scholarships
- Company sponsorship
- Loans (friends, family, bank)
- Fundraising (Venture capitalist etc.)

The option you pursue will largely depend on how much money you need. If you just need a few thousand dollars, you can probably borrow money from someone or save the money. If you need tens of thousands of dollars you might start thinking of ways to obtain a bank loan, a grant or a scholarship. If you need hundreds of thousands of dollars, you'll probably require the support of venture capitalists.

Now, what about you? What would be the best way to obtain the money you need?

An important question to ask yourself is, who could benefit from helping you? Is your business serving a cause people or organizations would want to support? Some examples would be:

- Gender equality

- Environmental issues
- Animals' rights
- Local communities support
- Education, and
- Poverty relief.

You may find companies, local governments or organizations willing to support you for PR purposes or because they support your mission.

7. Getting more money

Another way you can obtain the money you need is simply by saving and/or earning more. Pretty straightforward. To save more money can you reduce some expenses? For instance, you could:

- Move to a more affordable place
- Go out less often, or
- Only purchase things you absolutely need.

Exercise:

To save more money it is important you know exactly where all your money goes. For thirty days, keep all your receipts and record every expense. Then look over them and see where you can reduce your overheads. For instance, to make more money you could:

- Ask for a raise/promotion
- Do overtime
- Work another job at night or during the weekend, and/or
- Start getting paid for your passion—if you've already

developed valuable skills, why not try using them to generate an income?

Final tip: Avoid focusing solely on saving money. There is potentially no ceiling on how much money you can make, but there is only so much money you can save. It is easier to save more money—and still buy things you want—when you make more money!

* * *

Action step

Complete the exercise in the action guide (*Part 6. - Finding money*).

22

FINDING INFORMATION

As I've mentioned before, nowadays you have access to all the information you'll ever need. You have no excuse not to learn what you need to achieve your goal. Whatever your career goal is, make sure you learn everything there is to know. Strive to become as knowledgeable as the people in the industry you want to work in. Don't be the person who talks about opening a restaurant but hasn't read a single book on the topic or talked to any restauranteurs. Know your stuff and people will start trusting you. Some might even help you.

You can learn anything

To design your ideal career and life, the key is to realize you can learn anything. If you're truly motivated and willing to take action on the information you research, you can acquire any skill you need at very low cost. It doesn't matter if it's computer programming, Chinese, marketing, graphic design or coaching. With the information available online or in your local library, there is no limit to what you can learn.

Books: reading books is an excellent way to learn from experts who spend decades researching specific topics. You can absorb decades of experience in a few hours.

Videos: YouTube and other similar websites offer millions of videos on virtually anything from how to repair your washing machine to how to become a CIA agent, (yes, I actually typed these words in the YouTube search bar).

Blogs: There are millions of blogs and some of them can be extremely useful. Note that the quality and depth of the information provided may vary, though.

Online courses: Online courses can be a great way to study topics in more depth. Courses tend to be well-structured and well-organized, which can greatly facilitate your learning. You'll find all prices, from free courses to high-end courses that sell for thousands of dollars. Udemy.com is a great place to start. I regularly buy courses from the site.

N.B. make sure you wait for promotions when most of the courses are available for $10—they usually run several of these promotions throughout the year.

Facebook groups and forums: Facebook groups can be a great way to find like-minded people and keep your motivation high. You can also learn from other people's questions or ask your own. I highly recommend you look for the best Facebook groups related to your career goal and join them. I have greatly benefitted from joining Facebook groups for writers.

Action step

Make a list of books, blogs, videos, online courses and Facebook groups/forums that would give you the best information possible.

Adopting a mastery mindset

This is essential to achieving your life and career goals. Put simply, adopting a mastery mindset means knowing how to learn. Most people do not go deep enough when they learn. They stay at the surface. They are too eager to learn and often miss the fundamentals, and mastering the fundamentals is critical to success in any endeavor. High-achievers and professional athletes know this very well. The best in the world often go back to the basics when they want to improve. As Bruce Lee once said, *"I fear not the man who has practiced ten thousand kicks once, but I fear the man who has practiced one kick ten thousand times."* True experts know the importance of mastering the fundamentals and practice again and again until they achieve results they want. Do you?

Five obstacles to developing a mastery mindset

1. Shiny Object Syndrome

One of the main reasons people fail to achieve their goals is they spread themselves to thin. They become distracted by trying to accomplish too many things at once and end up either achieving nothing or obtaining mediocre results at best. A far better strategy is to focus on one or two skills/business ideas and obtain satisfying results before expanding your horizon. If you look closely, this is what most successful people do. They implement one major business idea successfully before they even consider expanding their business. The good news is once you achieve tangible results in one area, you can often recreate similar results in other areas of life.

2. Lack of patience

Another fundamental reason people do not achieve their goals is lack of patience. It comes from the inability to expend the effort and time needed to reach the desire outcome. To develop a mastery mindset, you must accept that anything worth pursuing takes time and effort. Also, remember there is always a lag between the time you sow the seed and the time the plant starts growing.

3. The "*I Already Know That*" Syndrome

Most people mistake intellectual knowledge for real knowledge. Knowing something intellectually doesn't mean you have mastered it. We all have friends who seem to know everything about a specific topic such as how to create a business, how to approach women or how to make more money. However, when you have a closer look, you quickly realize they aren't walking the talk. Knowing you should exercise every day isn't the same thing as actually doing it. Each time you catch yourself saying or thinking, "*I already know that,*" ask yourself whether you are a living proof of it.

4. Pride

Have you ever been too proud to acknowledge the fact you don't know how to do something? Pride can be a dangerous thing as it can prevent you learning what is necessary to achieve your life and career goals. If pride has stopped you learning something essential to your business or life plan, now might be the time to swallow this pride.

5. Complacency

It is not a bad thing to feel good about your skills and abilities. However, it becomes a problem when you adopt the attitude you don't need to learn anything new. This leads to complacency. I can guarantee you the top performers in your industry are constantly looking for ways to improve, and so should you. I believe it is essential to find a healthy balance between feeling confident in what you do, and continuously striving to improve your performance. Always assume there is more too learn, and ask yourself how you can become even better. Finally, remember you don't know what you don't know. And trust me, there are plenty of things you and I don't know, (yet).

For a more in-depth explanation on the Mastery Mindset, I recommend you check out my book, *The One Goal: Master the Art of Goal Setting, Win Your Inner Battles, and Achieve Exceptional Results.*

* * *

Action step

Complete the exercise in the action guide (*Part 6. - Finding information*).

23

FINDING THE TIME

Time is the most important resource you have. It's more important than anything else—including money. You can always make more money, but you can never make more time. Each second passed is gone forever. Sadly, most of us waste our time. The average American watches several hours of TV each day (up to five hours according to some surveys). It's as though we have failed to understand how precious our time is. To design your ideal career and ideal life you must start claiming your time back. This includes, reducing the time you spent watching TV and saying no to anything that isn't aligned with your values and mission.

Creating a time log

How much time can you dedicate to your career goal each day? Many people complain they don't have enough time. The fact is we all have 24 hours in a day. Some use their time to build a fortune and a career and life they love, others waste it, and end up wondering why they're not where they want to be. Which group do you belong to? Which group do you *want to* belong to?

The first step to reclaiming your time is to know exactly how you use it. The time log exercise will help you just do this. To complete the exercise, record everything you do for an entire week. This may sound tedious, but it will serve you well in the future. Use your notebook, your computer or a sheet of paper and write down each activity you engage in and how much time you spend on it. Do it/this in real time to make sure you don't forget anything. You should include everything you do, including:

- What you do at work
- Breakfast/lunch/dinner
- TV/leisure time, and
- Commuting, etc.

By the end of the week, you should have a clear idea of the way you use your time. Now, ask the following:

- What percentage do you spend in productive work (be honest)?
- How much TV/leisure time do you allow yourself?

Is it true you really don't have time? Is it true you can't commit any time to changing your career and life for the better?

To design your dream career, it is essential you respect your time and treat it as the most important asset you have. Bill Gates schedules appointments and tasks in six minutes increments. What does it say about his relationship with time? When you look at highly successful people, you'll notice they have a totally different relationship with time. While most people use their valuable time (a scarce resource) to save a few dollars (an abundant resource), wealthy people do the opposite: they use their money to save their precious time.

Another great example of a poor use of time is staying at a job you hate for forty years just to make a living. You're basically trading your precious time, a finite resource, for money, a virtually unlimited resource. This is what most people do. You might say, money might be unlimited when you make tons of it, but for me it is damn scarce! I got it. The point is you should enjoy your time *and* make money doing so. You shouldn't simply trade your time for money. That's what creating your ideal career is all about. As Confucius allegedly said, *"Choose a job you love, and you will never work a day in your life."*

The opportunity cost of time

When you watch TV, you automatically say no to working on your side business or educating yourself. When you volunteer for something you're not interested in, you miss an opportunity to use your time to work on a project you're deeply passionate about. Can you see the opportunity lost here? I want you to realize that each time you say no to an activity that is aligned with your purpose and values, you're doing a disservice to yourself and, most likely, to others.

The reason it's important you know your core values and purpose is to allow you to organize your entire life around them. When you do so, taking decisions becomes much easier and you will feel better about yourself.

I know what I want and decide what to do based on that knowledge. For instance, freedom is one of the most important values for me. Thus, when new opportunities arise, I always ask myself whether they will help me create more freedom in my life or limit my freedom.

- If I do this, will I be able to work from anywhere in the world, whenever I want?
- Does it require me to trade my time for money or is it an activity that can generate passive income for years to come?

These are the two main questions I ask myself each time I need to make a decision. Anything that doesn't allow me to design my ideal life is usually a "No" for me. I encourage you to do the same. Whatever you do each day is either moving you closer to your ideal career and life or away from it. So, make sure most of what you do is geared toward creating a life you love.

Refer to the action guide and use the time log sheet to record what you do for an entire week.

✶ ✶ ✶

Action step

Complete the exercise in the action guide (*Part 6. - Finding the time*).

PART VII

MAKING IT HAPPEN

24

CREATING AN ACTION PLAN

To turn your goal into reality you need to put a specific action plan in place. For now, let's focus on your major career goal. If you would like to pursue several goals simultaneously, simply repeat the following process for each one.

1. Creating a list of tasks

The first step is to write down all the tasks you need to complete to achieve your goal. Include everything you can think of. Focus on the big picture and identify the key milestones you must go through to attain your ultimate goal.

If you don't know all the tasks your goal involves, do your research. Start by searching for general articles on how to achieve your goal. This will give you the big picture. Then, look for more in-depth articles or books if needed. Whenever possible, talk to people who have the career you want. It will cut through the noise, saving you a lot of time and effort. Simply ask them what you need to do to build a similar career.

As you conduct more research, keep adding tasks to your list.

Spend a few days to come up with an exhaustive list. You might want to set a clear deadline and add, "creating a specific plan," as the first step on your list. Planning well will save you time later. The success expert, Brian Tracy, goes as far as saying each minute spent in planning saves ten minutes in execution.

Milestones will vary based on your goal. Some examples are:

- Contacting your network
- Creating a business plan
- Creating a product or service
- Designing a website
- Finding an internship
- Finding a mentor
- Obtaining a scholarship
- Having an interview with a person in your field of interest
- Hiring a coach
- Learning a specific skill, and
- Preparing for an exam, etc.

For each milestone, identify the tasks you need to complete before you can reach it. You can use a mind map (spider diagram) to do so (as we did for previous exercises). You now have an overview of most of the tasks you must complete to design your ideal career. (Feel free to use the mind map template I've included in the action guide).

Action step

Complete the exercise in the action guide (*Part 7. - Creating an action plan*).

2. Strategizing

Now you have an exhaustive list of tasks, it is time to strategize. Look at your career goal and ask yourself the following questions:

*a) What **core skills** must I master to achieve my goal?*

Most career goals require you to master new skills or improve your current skill set. Write down the fundamental skills you must develop to achieve your goal. These could include job interview skills, writing skills, technical skills or networking skills.

*b) What are the **Key Success Factors** for that goal? What will determine whether I will achieve it or not?*

Each goal has Key Success Factors that determine whether you will achieve your goal. Identifying them is critical. For instance, I believe the Key Success Factors for my goal of making a living from my writing are:

1. Writing and publishing quality books on a regular basis.
2. Collaborating with other authors/bloggers: Having a network of authors/bloggers who can help me promote my work.
3. Marketing my books on a daily basis: Mastering Amazon Marketing Services, Facebook ads and other book promotion ads services, tweaking my book descriptions, and so on.

While there are other factors, these are the ones I've identified as the Key Success Factors for my goal.

Your turn now. What are the Key Success Factors for your goal?

*c) What are the **worst-case scenarios** I could encounter? How do I plan to deal with them?*

By identifying all the things that may go wrong you'll improve your resilience and significantly increase your chances of success. For the sake of this exercise I encourage you to think of the worst-case scenarios and write them down.

Some examples of worst-case scenarios are:

- Failing to make any money from your business in the first six months/year/two years
- Not receiving any support from family or friends, and
- Lacking money to receive training or purchase what you need to achieve your goal.

Spend a couple of minutes to visualize yourself going through your worst-case scenarios. Use the 'Stoic Approach' and feel the pain and the frustration. Imagine not making any money for months. Imagine your friends and family not believing in you. Imagine yourself on the verge of giving up.

Now, make a promise to yourself that you will not let any of these obstacles prevent you from achieving your goal. Accept these challenges as part of the journey. They are the downs needed for you to go up. These are normal things that happen to anyone who chooses to go after what he or she wants. Treat them as such. Remember, if you don't feel like giving up from time to time, you probably not pursuing your real goals. The journey towards a worthy goal can be pretty challenging.

*d) How can I achieve the goal **faster**?*

The purpose of this question is to identify high-impact actions. The 80/20 rule states that 80% of our results come from 20% of our actions. What are these 20% actions for you? To help you identify these actions you can ask yourself the following questions:

- What would I do if I had only one month to achieve my goal? What about one week?

- If I could do no more than three things every day to move toward my goal, what would they be? If I could do only one thing what would it be?
- If achieving my goal was a matter of life and death, what would I do differently?

Another great question is from the popular book *The One Thing*, by Gary Keller:

What's the ONE Thing I could do, such that by doing it, everything else would be easier or unnecessary?

*e) What could I do **every day** to increase the chances of achieving my goal?*

This will help you identify the few key actions or habits that move the needle toward the 'success' mark. The results we accomplish in life result from what we do every day. People who implement powerful daily habits and stay consistent with them long-term are the ones who end up being the most successful. If you want to know where you'll likely end up in ten years, ask yourself the following question:

If I keep doing what I'm doing today/this week and maintain the same daily habits where will I be in ten years?

Answering this question with pure raw honesty will tell you a lot. You can go one step further and ask yourself this question for each area of your life. If you keep doing what you're doing today/this week, where will you be in ten years in the following areas:

- Your career
- Your family life
- Your finances
- Your health
- Your level of fulfillment

- Your personal growth
- Your relations, and
- Your spirituality.

Powerful question, isn't it?

Action step

Complete the exercise in the action guide (*Part 7. - Strategizing*).

3. Creating powerful daily habits

One effective way to answer the above question with confidence and know you will likely end up where you want to be is to have consistent daily habits in line with your Key Success Factors. To use the same example as before, my Key Success factors are:

1. Writing books
2. Connecting with other authors/bloggers, and
3. Marketing my books.

Now, to answer the question, *"If I keep doing what I'm doing today, will I be where I want to be ten years from now?"* I would have to answer yes to the following questions:

1. Did I write today?
2. Did I contact other authors or bloggers today?
3. Did I promote my book today?

If I can answer yes to these three questions, I'm probably on the right track.

Does it sound too simple? Below are some explanations to illustrate how I came to this conclusion:

1. Writing daily

Successful authors are extremely consistent with their writing routine. For instance, Stephen King writes every day including birthdays and holidays. His goal is to write at least 2,000 words per day. Many other authors write every day either for a set period of time or until they write a specific number of words.

2. Networking

I've noticed successful self-published authors have created meaningful connections with other authors from whom they can receive help when they release a book. One of my fellow writers told me the number one reason he's been successful writing books is related to the network he built over the years. If I were to contact just one person every day, over a year I would have reached out to 365 people.

3. Book promotion

Jack Canfield, author of the popular series, *Chicken Soup for the Soul,* did at least five things every day to promote his book. It took over a year before the book sales took off and his book was rejected by 144 publishers.

Now, your Key Success Factors will be different from mine, but whether you want to create your own business or land your dream job, there will be specific tasks that, when done every day, will move you closer to your goal. Your daily habits will likely include the following:

- Contacting other people. You will have to reach out to people in your industry. It could be to find potential partners for your business or to connect with decision makers who can offer you a job. When it comes to finding your dream job, it is far more effective to connect with people who can directly hire you than to merely send resumes by the dozen.

- Developing your skills. Whether you want to create your own business or work for a company, you will need to develop several key skills. Making sure you improve your skill set every day will significantly increase your chances of success.

What could you do to turn your Key Success Factors into daily habits?

For a simple step-by-step method to create long-lasting habits that will change your life, refer to my book *"Habits That Stick: The Ultimate Guide to Building Habits That Sticks Once and For All."*

* * *

Action step

Complete the exercise in the action guide (*Part 7. - Creating powerful daily habits*).

4. Scheduling

Now you have a clear goal, and have identified the tasks, milestones and Key Success Factors, it is time to create a specific schedule for your goal.

Scheduling is not a perfect science. As you work toward your goal, many things can happen, and it may take you much longer than you expect to achieve your goal. The key is to identify major milestones and track your progress based on these milestones. You can adjust your plan over time to take changing circumstances into account.

Now, take a pen and a **piece** of paper (A3 size if possible), and add vertical lines to separate each month. If you believe you can reach your goal in less than ninety days, divide the chart into weeks.

Feel free to use the template I've included in your free downloadable Dream Career Action Guide.

Add your milestones to the schedule. I recommend you multiply your original timeframe by 1.5 or 2 to make it more realistic.

Then, below each milestone write down corresponding tasks. From now on, you'll refer to this schedule every day. Make sure you put it on your desk or somewhere you can see it regularly.

Take a few seconds to celebrate. It is not a small accomplishment. Did you know only a few people have written goals and even fewer look at them every day? Thus, just by setting goals, creating a plan and reading it daily, you'll already ahead of ninety-five percent of the population.

Action step

Complete the exercise in the action guide (*Part 7. - Scheduling*).

5. Just getting started

Have you ever heard your friends or colleagues talk about their dream to one day own a shop? How many of them actually took the first step? I suspect only a fraction of the population will ever take the first step toward their biggest dream.

The truth is, achieving big goals doesn't require you to do extraordinary things. The small steps you take consistently every day lead to long-term results. As Henry Ford said, *"Nothing is particularly hard if you divide it into small jobs."*

Now, look at this month's tasks in your schedule and ask yourself, "What small step can I take today?" Then do it. It doesn't have to be anything big. It could be as simple as writing an email, calling a friend or buying a book. Find the one task that inspires you the most and start working on it today.

Then, take one more step tomorrow and the day after. I recommend you take one simple action every day during the first seven days to start building momentum. Consistency helps build motivation and, over time, it will boost your self-confidence.

Action step

Complete the exercise in the action guide (*Part 7. - Just getting started*)

25

SETTING GOALS

Now you have created a plan, let's write down more specific goals. I recommend you break your long-term goal into yearly, quarterly, monthly, weekly and daily goals.

To set goals, we'll simply use the milestones you already put in your plan. For daily and weekly goals select the tasks you've written down and assign them to a specific week. If needed, break these tasks down even further.

I understand that if you have never set written goals before, it may sound overwhelming. Don't worry though. Start by setting yearly, quarterly and monthly goals based on your milestones. You'll find that weekly and daily goals come naturally. All you have to do is to break down your larger goals into smaller ones.

Setting weekly goals

To set weekly goals, ask yourself, what could you accomplish this week, to make it a great week? What would really move the needle forward? Try to aim for three to six goals.

Setting daily goals

To set daily goals look at your list of weekly goals and further break them down whenever relevant. Add other tasks you want to complete that day if needed. Again, aim at three to six daily goals, and this includes your Key Success Factors.

The most effective way to set daily goals is to plan your day the previous night. Before going to bed, make it a habit to spend a few minutes to think of what you want to accomplish the next day, and create a list. Alternatively, you can plan your day first thing in the morning. This habit alone will boost your productivity and significantly increase your chances of reaching your goal.

To write down your goals you can use a simple notebook or an agenda. No need for fancy tools. Just use a new page each day to write your daily goals. You can also use the template in your action guide.

For a step-by-step process on how to set goals, refer to my book *Goal Setting: The Ultimate Guide to Achieving Life-Changing Goals.*

Action step

Complete the exercise in the action guide (*Part 7. - Setting goals*).

26

BUILDING ACCOUNTABILITY

Are you committed to achieving your goal? If so, putting in place an accountability system will further help you reach your commitments in the long-term.

We tend to take more action and move faster when we have someone who keeps us accountable. This is one of the roles performed by a coach for instance. If you want to maximize your chances of success, you must have some sort of accountability.

To know whether you have such a system right now, simply ask yourself, who will call me out if I don't do what I said I would do? If the answer is nobody, then you don't have an effective or reliable accountability system.

Select the right accountability partner

Having an accountability partner is an effective way to stay on track with your goal. However, you have to ensure your accountability partner is willing to call you out. You also want them to be disciplined. Avoid partnering with someone who can't keep their word. Ideally, your partner should be one of the most disciplined and self-motivated person you know. Finally, when you face challenges, your accountability partner should encourage you, not put you down.

Here is a great question to help you identify your accountability partner: "If I needed an important job to get done—and it was a matter of life and death—who would I entrust to get the task done?" This person would likely make a great accountability partner.

A good idea is to find someone who isn't a close friend, which can prevent your meetings becoming too casual. I don't know about you, but I can't think of many friends with whom this kind of accountability partnership would work.

I also encourage you to join my Facebook group, *Discover What You Love and Make it Happen*, and connect with other like-minded people who want an accountability partner.

Finding the right partner might take some time. Often, people will become busy. As a result, the whole accountability system can fall off after a couple of months. Bear this in mind as you look for your accountability partner.

To create a fruitful long-term relationship with your partner, it is important you follow a specific guideline.

How to create an effective accountability system

Think of it as a contract between two people. And, as any contract:

1. **It has to be agreed**. You both have to agree with the terms of the contract. This means you both must believe the terms are reasonable and are confident you can follow through to the end.
2. **You have to commit to the partnership and the**

goals. You must be willing to respect the contract conditions and to pay the consequences when you don't. Remember, your accountability partner is not your friend, (at least not during your accountability meeting).

3. **It has to be specific**. It should lay out exactly what you will do, when and how. For an accountability system to be effective it must include the following points:

- How you will communicate, (email, phone, Skype, in person etc.).
- How often (once a day/week/month).
- How long you'll work together, (it's a good idea to stay together until the deadline of one of a key milestone. Ideally, at least three months).
- What exactly you'll do during each session.
- What the consequences will be if you don't follow through.
- How you will reward yourself when you follow through.

Once you have the right partner and the right system in place, you will benefit greatly from your accountability system. I'm self-motivated and can do pretty well without anybody else's support, but I still benefit from such a system, and I believe you will too.

A specific example of accountability

Now, let me give you a specific example of what the first meeting with your partner could look like.

1. Set a first meeting/Skype/FaceTime call with your partner.

2. Clarify the following points:

- Expectations. Ask each other what you except from your partner. For instance, you can ask the following questions

a. Let's say everything works perfectly well between us, what would be the ideal outcome for you?

b. How can I best help you? You can also mention how you like to be encouraged. Some people prefer to be gently encouraged, while others prefer to be pushed.

c. What do you want to accomplish in the next year/five years? It's a good idea to learn more about the other person's long-term vision and goals. This way, you'll be better equipped to help them during brainstorming sessions.

- When you will meet. Set a specific day and time. For me, the best times to meet are the beginning or end of the week. Make sure you treat the meeting as you would do with an appointment with the doctor. I recommend meeting/talking once a week.

- What the agenda will be. Decide how you will use the time you spend together—I recommend a one-hour-long meeting. You can split the session in two and allocate thirty minutes for each.

During the first five minutes you'll discuss your past week—what you did and didn't accomplish. Then, you'll talk about some of the challenges you had: procrastination, lack of motivation, unexpected events, mental blocks etc. If you feel the need to vent, feel free to do so but limit it to five to ten minutes maximum. If you are the one listening, avoid trying to "fix" your partner or offer solutions. Do your best to listen with compassion and avoid judging them. Wait for your partner to finish before moving on to the brainstorming/suggestions session.

Finally, you can spend a few minutes at the end to share your goals.

- How long you will work together. Share some of your goals and agree on the initial duration of the partnership. Three months or more is preferable. If it works well, you can extend the agreement for as long as you want. A good practice is to stay together until you each achieve one of your major goals or reach the deadline for that goal.

- When you will send your weekly goals to your partner. Send them before the meeting/call. That way you can share them and even commit to achieving during the meeting/call.

3. Write down your list of goals

Once the first meeting is over write down your list of goals. You can share your weekly, monthly and/or yearly goals.

4. Send your goals to your partner

Send your goals to your partner using the agreed means of communication. It could be either by email or using a software application like Asana (*create tutorial). Whenever you can, set a specific day for each task (especially for important tasks you're likely to procrastinate on).

Questions to ask during the meeting:

The partnership will be more effective if you know what questions to ask your partner. Below are some powerful questions I recommend you use during the meeting:

Reviewing past week goals:

- What went well this week?
- What could you have done better?
- What did you learn?
- What will you do better next time?
- What would you like to celebrate/acknowledge yourself for?

Brainstorming:

- What's holding you back?
- What are your options?

- Can you think of anything else?

Discussing next week goals:

- On a scale of 1 to 10 (where 10 is high and 1 is low), how confident are you that you will achieve the goal What's holding you back? What can you do about it?
- On a scale of 1 to 10 (where 10 is high and 1 is low), how committed are you to achieving this goal next week? Can you commit to this goal? Can you commit to achieve the goal on *add specific day*?

Bonus tip:

We often get stuck when we have too many open loops—things we haven't completed—or an important task we've been procrastinating on for a long time. An accountability partner I worked with in the past was finally able to finish laying the hallway floor in this house after I asked him whether he was willing to commit. This gave him a motivational boost and lead him to tackle many more tasks. This is the beauty of momentum. Try it for yourself.

When you work with your partner, try to complete the biggest task or project on your plate. During the first week, you can simply commit to finishing this one task.

Hiring a coach

If you're struggling to design an accountability system that works for you, you might choose to hire a coach. In addition to keeping you accountable, a coach will also help you shift your perspective, overcome mental blocks, organize your ideas, clarify what you really want and create a clear action plan, (among other things).

Joining a group

Being part of a group of like-minded people might also help you remain motivated and take action towards your goals. That's why I love the Facebook author group. As I mentioned before, you should seek out such groups, not only to remain motivated, but also to learn from each member.

However, you must realize the level of accountability from being part of such groups is not as high as when you have a dedicated accountability partner (medium to high) or hire a coach (high).

Ideally, you should have several ways to maintain accountability. That's what I do since I cannot wait for divine inspiration to write my books. I'm accountable to:

- My editor (I have a deadline for sending him my books)
- My readers/subscribers, (I sent them my 2018 goals), and
- My current accountability partner.

With such a system in place, I achieve most of my goals on time.

However, there is no need to put incredible pressure on your shoulders right away. Start by setting small goals. As you achieve these goals consistently, you'll feel more and more confident in your ability to set and achieve bigger goals. Stretch yourself a little, but don't overdo it. The point is not to beat yourself up when you fail to achieve your goals, as this would slow down your progress and make you more likely to give up.

You can join my Facebook group, *Discover what you love and make it happen*, here.

Additional resources:

When I work with my accountability partner, I like to use the free software, Asana. You can use it to write down your goals. You can set deadlines for each and even add comments. In addition, you can also make them visible to your accountability partner. This tool can be used for project management as well and includes paid options for people who want more functionality. However, for accountability purposes, the free version is more than enough.

In the next section, I will answer some common questions you may have when following your passion and creating your ideal career.

* * *

Action step

Complete the exercise in the action guide (*Part 7. - Building accountability*).

PART VIII

FREQUENTLY ASKED QUESTIONS

a) Should I quit my job to create my own business? If so, when?

Many coaches recommend you quit your job when you're making more money from your side business than from your day job. However, if you decide to quit your job even though your side business is not (yet) generating a decent amount of money, I would recommend your situation matches *all* the following:

- You've been working on your side business for at least two years.
- You have savings. Ideally, you can work full-time on your new venture for a couple of years or more without having to worry about money.
- Your spouse is on board. He or she is working and can support you to some extent, and/or he or she believes in your business idea.

What if you're only making a few hundred dollars a month from your side business and have little savings? To choose whether or when to quit your day job, consider the following:

- How do you feel about your current job? Are you neutral or do you hate it? If you're neutral, you might want to hang in on a little bit longer. Conversely, if every day is a struggle, quitting your job might be the right thing to do even if it means taking a little more risk.
- How confident are you about your new venture? You might not be making enough money with your business, but if you are ninety percent confident of success, you might want to take a leap of faith. Below are some criteria to help you assess how likely you are to succeed:

1. Your level of passion for your business. If you absolutely love your new business and *know* it is what you want to do for the rest of your life, you are significantly more likely to succeed
2. How long you've already spent working on your business. If you've been working on your new venture for at least two years while having a full-time job, it shows that you are really committed and have the self-discipline and consistency needed to succeed.
3. The feedback you receive about your work. If people have told you that what you do is great, you may be on the right path. The belief I hold is that, if one person loves what I do, then millions of people will do. I just need to find them. It's even better if: 1) some people have paid for what you do, and 2) they are strangers, i.e. they are not family or friends.
4. How many people are doing the same thing successfully. If tens of thousands of people are making a living doing the same thing, you're very likely to succeed as long as you remain consistent and do not give up. On the other hand, if only a handful of people are making money

doing it, it will be more challenging. It is then your job to be honest with yourself and analyze your chances of success and how much risk you're comfortable taking.

5. Your chance of finding a job if you fail in your new venture. Obviously, if you can go back to your previous job or easily find a job in your industry if you 'fail', you might as well jump right away. If not, it's your call to make. As a general rule, I believe you should learn new skills constantly and aim at financial confidence. That is, knowing you can make money no matter what. This includes developing valuable skills such as public speaking skills, leadership skills, marketing skills, and/or any technical skills in demand.

b) I still don't know what I love. What should I do?

Keep exploring different fields. Make sure you spend enough time to understand yourself and your personality. Do the exercises in this book one more time and keep tweaking your mission statement until you find something that really resonates with you. When you find something of interest, dig deeper. Often, when you become good at something you really start enjoying it. Finally, remember that finding what you love might take time. It took me several years to discover my dream career.

c) How do I know I'm on the right path?

Below are some signs to look for:

- It doesn't feel like work anymore.
- You feel as though you're making a difference in your own way.
- You genuinely believe you can do this thing for the rest of your life, or at least for many years to come.
- You are often in a state of flow and things come easily.

- You wonder if it's okay to be paid to do the work,
  (because it doesn't seem like work to you).

d) What if my passion changes over time?

Your passion may well change over time as your external
situation changes. However, your overall mission will generally
remain the same. This means you may change your job or career,
but it will still be part of your overall mission. For instance,
instead of writing books, I could choose to create a company that
helps young people find the right job and inspire them to be the
best they can be. My activity would be different, but my mission
would remain the same. Again, there is no right or wrong answer.
The key is to be honest with yourself and do what feels right
to you.

*e) How do I differentiate what should remain a hobby from what could
become a career?*

Sometimes, we stop enjoying something as soon as we receive
money for it. So, it might be worth reflecting on whether you
want to make money out of your passion or keep it as a hobby.

At the same time, if you really love something and can't stop
thinking about it all day long, you'll naturally want to spend most
of your time doing it. For instance, when I was still an employee,
I couldn't help but think, "I should be writing books, I should be
working on my online business. Why do I have to sit here doing
something I hate and something I am poor at when I could do
something I love and am good at?"

For me, my side job had become an obsession, and it was
definitely not just a hobby. What about you? How do you feel
about your passion?

f) How do I make a living from my passion?

First, you must see if there is a demand for what you do. It is easier to offer a product or service when there is already a demand for it than to try to create a new market, (even if the competition is fierce). Are people already paying for similar products? How many people are making money doing the exact thing you're doing? Is it possible to work for a company or would you need to set one up on your own?

Then, you want to look in details at what people in your field are doing. Analyzing your competition will allow you to create a clear action plan and also help you come up with a product or service that stands out.

It will help you define your unique selling proposition (USP). Your USP is what differentiates your product from any other product. The marketing strategist Jay Abraham defines an USP as, "*a distinct, appealing idea that sets your business apart from every other 'me too' competitor.*" Ask yourself why people would buy your product or service as opposed to other similar products? Do you have an attractive price? A high-quality product/service? A unique story behind your product/service?

Another obvious way to see whether there is demand for your service is to make your first sale. Are strangers willing to pay for your service? If you can find one of them, chances are there are many more out there.

To learn more about ways you can stand out from the competition check out Jay Abraham's book, *Getting Everything You Can Out of All You've Got: 21 Ways You Can Out-Think, Out-Perform and Out-Earn the Competition.*

g) How long will it take for me to make money from doing what I love?

This depends on many factors. If you build a business for scratch, apart from some exceptions, it could take several years.

If you look for the dream job, it could take you only a few months provided you invest enough time and effort into your job search and/or have relevant past experiences. In other cases, it could take much longer.

Remember, you'll spend a big chunk of your life at work and your job will play a large part in determining the quality of your life. If we assume a conservative 1,500 hours worked per year, over the span of a 40-year long career, you will have spent 60,000 hours working. The question is, what kind of work do you want to be doing for these 60,000 hours?

h) How do I know I will not regret my choice?

Sometimes we make mistakes. We make the wrong decisions and have to bear the consequences. To avoid having any regrets, project yourself into the future. Ask yourself the following question: When I reach eighty will I regret not having done that? If the answer is a clear yes, you know what you have to do. Remember, we often regret what we didn't do, not what we did.

i) Should I ever give up on my dream?

Let's first define what you mean by 'giving up' here. If you mean, not starting because you will likely fail, I would say never do it. You can always find a little time to work on your goal every day. So, if you have a dream, just take the first step. As you do so, you will build momentum, and as Newton's First Law states, an object in motion tends to stay in motion. This is also true for human beings. Keep moving towards your dream and see what happens.

If by giving up you mean, stop pursuing your dream because you didn't achieve the results you want, I would counter by offering the following quote from the personal development blogger Steve Pavlina:

> *In the long run, people usually do achieve their goals if they persist, stay flexible, and don't give up. The biggest challenge for most people is persisting long enough to win the mental game.*

Most people give up way too soon. As a result, they never reach their full potential. I thought of giving up many, many times in the past. I remember times when I told myself, "What's the point? Nobody is reading what I'm writing anyway. Why am I working so hard for nothing?"

One piece of advice I would give you is to never take the decision to give up when you're in a negative state of mind. Allow yourself to make a decision once you feel better. Decisions taken when we are sad, depressed or frustrated are seldom good ones.

Ask yourself if you will regret having given up. As long as you can feel an ounce of regret, I recommend you carry on. Use each setback as an opportunity to reflect. How could you improve? What you could do differently? I believe one of the most important qualities to develop is never-ending quest for self-improvement. Overcome your pride and never assume you know everything. Instead, be willing to learn and constantly look for pieces of the puzzle you may have missed. Sometimes, a slight change in what you do or the way you think can make all the difference in the world.

Finally, decide your threshold by determining exactly under what conditions you would give up. Refuse to give up unless these conditions are met.

j) How do I convince my spouse/family to support me?

Changing people or convincing them can be extremely challenging. Below are some of the things you can do:

- Make them your advisors. Instead of telling them your plan, tell them you've been thinking of some ideas and would like their opinion. Ask them what they would do if they were in your shoes. People are much more likely to support a plan they have contributed to.
- Don't convince them. Another approach is simply to

tell them what you've decided to do. They may not like it, but it's your choice. This technique will work better if your decision doesn't have a significant impact on your family. Obviously, if it requires you sell your house, quit your job and move to another country, you might want to avoid using that technique, (unless you're single).

- Show them results. Perhaps you have started working on your new business a few hours per week and now feel much happier, which benefits your family. Or maybe you find some clients or receive great feedback. Show the feedback to your family.
- Negotiate. If none of the above work, negotiate. Ask your family what would work for them. Find out what their main concerns are and see how you can work together to dissolve them.

k) How do I find time to work on my goals in my busy day-to-day life?

We discussed this earlier (*add segment reference*), but briefly, start valuing your time more. People are seldom/rarely so busy they don't have thirty minutes or one hour of free time per day. Make sure you completed the time log exercise and recorded how you use your time for an entire week. Below are some ideas to free up some time:

- Cut the time you spend watching TV.
- Go out less or less longer, (e.g. arrive later and leave early to carve out some time to work on your goal.
- Use commuting time wisely, (listen to audiobooks, brainstorm ideas etc.).
- Use your lunch break to work on your goal.
- Prepare meals in advance to reduce the time you spend eating.
- Hire a house cleaner.

- See if you can reduce your working hours, (although this might entail a reduction in salary).

These are just some ideas. Ideally, try to block out chunk of times to focus on your goal and schedule them each week. If your goal is really important, you *must* make the time for it.

l) How do I remain motivated and accountable long-term?

Even when you love what you do, it is easy to lose momentum. As Newton's First Law also states: an object at rest tends to stay at rest. This is why it is important you remain consistent and do your best to work on your goal every single day.

- Find an accountability partner. Re-read the chapter on accountability and follow the instructions. Don't forget to join my Facebook group, which will help you find an accountability partner.
- Focus on your process-goals. You might fail to achieve your result-goals but make sure you focus on your process-goals, (goals you have control over). These are goals such as writing a certain number of words per day or jogging for a certain distance or duration.
- Implement a daily routine. Whenever possible, add tasks related to your Key Success Factors to your daily routine. As you keep taking action every day you will build and maintain momentum.
- Reassess the 'whys' behind your goal. Make sure you have enough compelling reasons for your goal. Remind yourself of all the reasons this goal is important to you. If you can't come up with anything compelling enough, perhaps you need to reframe your goal or choose a more exciting goal.
- Hire a coach. If you think hiring a coach would allow you to overcome some of your limiting beliefs and stay accountable, consider doing so.

m) What if I keep failing?

'Failure' is only a concept. I don't believe in failure. People who are successful in their field have an entirely different relationship to failure than most people.

'Failure' is nothing more than trying something without obtaining the results you wanted. It doesn't mean *you* are a failure. It doesn't mean you aren't good enough either. 'Failure' is simply feedback. It is part of the process we call success and is *not* separate from it. Regard 'failure' as a built-in feedback mechanism and part of the success process. Below is what I consider real failures:

- Letting 'failure' affect you too much. Taking 'failure' personally is a major issue many people face. You are *not* a failure! You simply tried something that didn't work out the way you wanted. Make it a habit to reframe 'failure'. Say to yourself, "I just tried something, and it didn't work out. Next."
- Receiving feedback ('failing') and not learning from it, (i.e. not changing anything in the way we operate). This usually happens when we have too much pride or prefer to play the victim rather than taking full responsibility and changing what needs to be changed. Your ability to learn from your failure will determine for a large part how successful you will be.
- Not 'failing'. Not trying anything because of fear of failure is a major mistake as well. Most successful people have 'failed' at least ten times more often than average people. If you don't 'fail' you will remain average. Accept the fact you cannot dissociate failure from success. They work hand in hand. See 'failure' as a necessary 'evil.'

n) How do I make my impossible dream happen? And should I?

Only *you* know whether you can make an impossible dream a reality. You may wonder whether the little voice within you encouraging you to pursue your dream is real or if you're just deluded. The only way for you to know is to trust your inner voice and chase your dream. Once you commit to making that dream a reality, use this book to create a plan, and work on developing an exceptional mindset. Remember the real battle is within.

o) I don't have any resources (connection or money). What should I do?

Your ultimate resource is your personal resourcefulness. If you have enough passion, drive, creativity, courage and persistence, you can obtain all the resources you need. Start by believing you can and will find a way to obtain any resource you need to achieve your goal. Then keep asking for what you need over and over.

Re-read this book and develop a powerful mindset. More importantly, take action consistently every day. Don't wait for the right resources to get started. Start in whatever way you can. Don't forget to brainstorm ways you can achieve your goal without (or with less of) the resources you believe you need. Finally, reevaluate the essence of your goal and see if you can achieve it by taking a different path.

p) What can I do to believe in myself more?

Confidence comes with experience. To believe more in yourself:

- Start by setting small daily goals and achieving them consistently.
- Buy a journal in which you write down all your accomplishments—small and big—and review it every day.
- Keep achieving small goals while acknowledging all your present and past accomplishments. Maintain this

momentum over the long-run to boost your confidence.

- Revisit your goal statement each day. Visualize yourself as having already achieved your goal.
- Do uncomfortable things on a regular basis to expand your zone of comfort.
- Surround yourself with positive people who believe in you and/or who have already achieved your goal, (offline or online).

q) What does it truly take to make my dream a reality?

To maximize the chances, you achieve your dreams you need:

- A crystal-clear understanding of what you want, (knowing exactly what your mission is)
- A strong sense of purpose behind your dreams, (having a big 'why' and strong emotional connections to it)
- A commitment to making it happen, (deciding it's going to happen. The only unknown is how much time it will take)
- Consistency over the long-term, (working on your goal every day)
- The ability to learn from your so-called failures, (taking one hundred percent responsibility both for your failures and your successes), and
- Continuous self-improvement, (a willingness to learn and set aside your pride).

r) I don't know what my strengths/talents are. What should I do?

Did you ask people around you? Make sure to ask your family, friends and colleagues. You can email people who know you well and ask them what they think your strengths are. You may be surprised by their answers.

Also, instead of searching for big strengths, look at anything you may be good at. These include things that may not appear significant to you at the moment. Avoid dismissing anything. A few seemingly insignificant strengths—when developed to their extreme and focused towards a worthy goal—can make a huge difference over time.

If you still struggle to identify your strengths, you can take skills assessment tests. I encourage you to start with StrengthsFinder 2.0 by Tom Wrath. It will help identify some of your core strengths.

CONCLUSION

Thank you for purchasing this book. Congratulations on reading until the end of the book. This shows me you are fully dedicated to creating a career and a life that you love.

By now, you've identified your strengths, passions and values as well as some of your key personality traits and you should have a better idea of what your ideal career looks like. You've also developed a strong mindset that enables you to make consistent progress toward your career goal until you achieve it. I guess, at this point, the only question I have left for you is:

Are you committed to designing your ideal career or are you merely interested?

Committing will make all the difference in the world. We usually know what to do but rarely do what we know. Don't read this book and forget about it. Keep moving toward your goal. If you haven't yet, go back and do the exercises and, more importantly, create your action plan.

Once you write down exactly what you want, create a plan of

action and resolve to make it happen, you can achieve extraordinary things.

I wish you all the best and hope to hear from you very soon. Feel free to contact me to share your story, ask me questions or simply say "hi."

I'm always delighted to receive emails from my readers.

I look forward to hearing from you very soon.

Warm regards,

Thibaut Meurisse

Founder of Whatispersonaldevelopment.org

What do you think?

I want to hear from you! Your thoughts and comments are important to me. If you enjoyed this book or found it useful **I'd be very grateful if you'd post a short review on Amazon or Goodreads**. Your support really does make a difference. I read all the reviews personally so that I can get your feedback and make this book even better.

Thanks again for your support!

OTHER BOOKS BY THE AUTHORS:

Goal Setting: The Ultimate Guide to Achieving Life-Changing Goals (Free Workbook Included)

Habits That Stick: The Ultimate Guide to Building Habits That Stick Once and For All (Free Workbook Included)

Master Your Emotions: A Practical Guide to Overcome Negativity and Better Manage Your Feelings (Free Workbook Included)

Productivity Beast: An Unconventional Guide to Getting Things Done (Free Workbook Included)

The Greatness Manifesto: Overcome Your Fear and Go After What You Really Want

The One Goal: Master the Art of Goal Setting, Win Your Inner Battles, and Achieve Exceptional Results (Free Workbook Included)

The Thriving Introvert: Embrace the Gift of Introversion and Live the Life You Were Meant to Live (Free Workbook Included)

Upgrade Yourself: Simple Strategies to Transform Your Mindset, Improve Your Habits and Change Your Life

Wake Up Call: How To Take Control Of Your Morning And Transform Your Life (Free Workbook Included)

ABOUT THE AUTHOR

THIBAUT MEURISSE

Thibaut Meurisse is a personal development blogger, author, and founder of whatispersonaldevelopment.org.

He has been featured on major personal development websites such as Lifehack, Goalcast, TinyBuddha, Addicted2Success, MotivationGrid or PickTheBrain.

Obsessed with self-improvement and fascinated by the power of the brain, his personal mission is to help people realize their full potential and reach higher levels of fulfillment and consciousness.

In love with foreign languages, he is French, writes in English, and lived in Japan for almost a decade.

Learn more about Thibaut at:

amazon.com/author/thibautmeurisse

whatispersonaldevelopment.org
thibaut.meurisse@gmail.com

GOAL SETTING BOOK PREVIEW

Introduction

Mr. Rohn, let me see your current list of goals. I've had a lot of experience and I've been out here for a while, so let's go over them and maybe I can really give you some good ideas." And I said, "I don't have a list." He said, " Well, if you don't have a list of your goals, I can guess your bank balance within a few hundred dollars." And he did.

—JIM ROHN, THE JIM ROHN GUIDE TO GOAL SETTING

I would like to thank you for downloading this e-book. In doing so, you have already shown your commitment to bettering your life by setting goals that truly excite you. You have joined those who have made the decision to take more control over their lives and give less power to circumstances. It's important to think about what where you want to be, whether it's one month, six months, one year, five years or even a decade or more from now.

Taking the time to identify the goals you wish to accomplish is the best way to make sure that you're going into the right direction. It will also keep you from pursuing goals that won't fulfill you.

Deciding to set goals is probably one of the most important decisions you can make, but most people don't set clear goals in their life. It's almost as if they believe they have no control over their life. As such, they wander through life heavily influenced by the circumstances and people around them. They give their power away to their environments instead of using it to create the lives they desire. They achieve far les than they would if they took the time to plan their lives and set specific goals.

Keep in mind, however, that having goals in and of itself is not enough. In fact, having goals that are unclear or out of alignment with what you want can be almost as bad as having none at all. Unfortunately, many goal setters spend years in dogged pursuit of a particular goal only to achieve it and realize that isn't what they genuinely wanted. This e-book will help you avoid that. Setting specific goals is one of the best decisions I've made in my life and the information within this book will give you an opportunity to do the same.

I first created a list of goals back in September of 2014 while in the process of building my website. Looking back, I often wonder why I'd never done it before and why I never learned about it in school. Setting goals is par for the course when it comes to personal development, however.

I believe that we all have the potential to accomplish great things in life. However, many of us never learned to tap into our intrinsic ability to self-motivate. We spend our childhoods studying to get good grades and trying to fit in in an attempt to please our parents, teachers, and peers. We then spend our adulthoods working for money and other external motivators. Our tendency to rely upon outside motivators is ironic considering how ineffective they are. Studies show that extrinsic motivators such as money are less efficient than intrinsic motivators like autonomy, self-mastery, or finding purpose. The carrot and stick approach is still in frequent use these days, but it's far from ideal. The reality is that intrinsic motivation yields better results and provides a greater sense of fulfillment than extrinsic motivation does.

Fortunately, learning to set the right goals will help you tap into your intrinsic motivation and allow you to uncover your hidden potential. This book is intended to help you figure out what you want to achieve and the kind of life you wish to create for yourself. I want you to set goals that inspire you, stir your soul, and make you want to jump out of bed every morning. Goal setting might seem intimidating, but it's more than worth it!

What you will learn in this book:

Within this book, you'll find a comprehensive method to achieve your goals. You won't just learn how to set goals effectively, you'll also learn to think better thoughts, overcome obstacles, and persevere until you reach your goal.

This Book Will:

1) Give you the opportunity to discover and set goals that genuinely matter to you

2) Help you set short-term, mid-term, and long-term goals in multiple areas of your life.

3) Help you realize your potential and achieve more than you thought possible.

4) Provide you with an effective strategy to achieve the goals you set.

5) Enable you to avoid the obstacles you will encounter while working towards your goals.

This book is full of valuable information, but remember that how much you get out of it is largely dependent upon how committed you are to implementing it. The ball is in your court!

I. Why goal setting is important

People without goals are doomed to work forever for people who do have goals.

— BRIAN TRACY.

Setting goals gives direction to your subconscious mind

Your automatic creative mechanism is teleological. That is, it operates in terms of goals and end results. Once you give it a definite goal to achieve, you can depend upon its automatic guidance system to take you to that goal much better than "you" ever could by conscious thought. "You" supply the goal by thinking in terms of end results. Your automatic mechanism them supplies the means whereby.

— MAXWELL MALTZ.

Did you know your subconscious mind could help you achieve your goal? Setting goals gives you a direction in life, but vague goals like making more money or being happy won't lead to a fulfilling life. Your subconscious mind is like a powerful machine, and understanding how it works is a big part of successful goal setting. Hypnotherapist Joseph Clough compares it to a GPS whereas Maxwell Maltz, author of Psycho-Cybernetics, calls it a mechanical goal-seeking device. If you put an address into your GPS, it will do whatever it can to reach your destination. The subconscious mind behaves similarly. Have you ever learned a new word only to find yourself hearing it everywhere you go? That's an example of your brain "priming". In other words, it's scanning your environment for all information relevant to the word, phrase, or details you've given it. As such, setting clear goals gives you a greater chance of accomplishing them. It sends a strong signal to your subconscious mind, which allows it to unleash its focusing power and look for any opportunities to achieve the goal. We talk more about the importance of specific goals later.

Setting goals empowers you

If you don't design your own life plan, chances are you'll fall into someone else's plan. And guess what they have planned for you? Not much.

—JIM ROHN.

Are you the one choosing your goals? Or are others choosing them for you? When you start setting intentions, you stop giving away your power.

When you start setting objectives in all the main areas of your life such as finances, relationships, career, and health, you stop giving power away and start empowering yourself. You make a conscious choice to become the creator of your life and begin to take responsibility in every aspect of your life.

Imagine the difference it would make in your life if you were to take the time to figure out your goals for the future. If you knew how much you wanted to earn in five years, how long you wanted to live, and where you'd like to be in twenty years, what would you do differently?

Setting goals increases self-esteem

High self-esteem seeks the challenge and stimulation of worthwhile and demanding goals. Reaching such goals nurtures good self-esteem. Low self-esteem seeks the safety of the familiar and undemanding. Confining oneself to the familiar and undemanding serves to weaken self-esteem.

— NATHANIEL BRANDEN.

Did you know that you could increase your self-esteem by setting clear goals? It's worth mentioning that having clear goals and achieving them builds and reinforces our self-esteem. In fact, Nathaniel Branden (author of *The Six Pillars Of Self-Esteem*) states that part of our self-esteem comes from a "disposition to experience ourselves as competent to cope with life's challenges". With every achievement we accomplish, we feel better equipped to deal with other goals and life challenges. In *The Pursuit of Happiness* David G. Myers shows that high self-esteem is one of the best predictors of personal happiness. Consistently accomplishing the goals you set is one of the most efficient ways to build self-esteem.

Goal setting changes your reality

The value of goals is not in the future they describe, but the change in perception of reality they foster

— DAVID ALLEN, GETTING THINGS DONE

Setting goals is a valuable process on its own, regardless of whether or not you'll achieve them. You're probably wondering why that's the case. Well, there are several reasons. Goal setting helps you think about your future, gives you an opportunity to reflect on your values, and helps you discover what matters most. It will bring clarity and allow you to see the bigger picture of your life. It doesn't get much more valuable than that.

Setting goals will also allow you to reconstruct your reality and realize that dreams you previously thought unattainable are in fact achievable. It all starts with identifying your real desires, no matter how ambitious they are. In so doing, you'll begin the process of overcoming your limiting beliefs. Limiting beliefs stem from past experiences and make it harder to get the life you want. You'll soon realize how restrictive limiting beliefs are and just how many of them stem from repetitive messages received from family, friends, and the media.

Lastly, goal setting will give you the opportunity to assess your current situation and close the gap between where you are and where you want to be.

Setting goals is good for your health

Use goals to live longer. No medicine in the world – and your physician will bear this out – is as powerful in bringing about life as is the desire to do something.

— David J. Schwartz, The Magic Of Thinking Big.

Dan Buettner, the author of *The Blue Zone: Lessons for Living Longer From the People Who've Lived The Longest,* identified 10 characteristics shared by those who live to 100. He identified "having a life purpose" as one of them. Setting goals that fully excite you is one of the best medicines and will work wonders for your health. An alarming number of people die within a few years of retirement. I believe this is partly because they no longer have exciting goals to motivate them, something that is especially likely for those who heavily identified with their job. What about you? Have you found goals that will motivate you well into old age?

How to set goals

The key to goal setting is for you to think on paper. Successful men and women think with a pen in their hands; unsuccessful people do not.

— BRIAN TRACY.

You can learn more at:

http://amazon.com/author/thibautmeurisse

Made in the USA
Columbia, SC
05 September 2018